WHEN THE SAINTS

GO HOBBLING IN:
EMMETT JAY SCOTT
AND THE BOOKER T. WASHINGTON MOVEMENT

BY MACEO CRENSHAW DAILEY, JR.

WHEN THE SAINTS
GO HOBBLING IN:
EMMETT JAY SCOTT
AND THE BOOKER T. WASHINGTON MOVEMENT

BY MACEO CRENSHAW DAILEY, JR.

SWEET EARTH FLYING PRESS

When the Saints Go Hobbling in: Emmett Jay Scott and the Booker T. Washington Movement ©
2013 By Maceo Crenshaw Dailey, Jr.

Published by Sweet Earth Flying Press LLC
508 Tawny Oaks Place
El Paso, Texas 79912

Book jacket and book design by Antonio Castro Graphic Design Studio

Library of Congress Control Number: 2013942284

ISBN: 978-0-9883331-1-6

Printed in the United States of America

Cover Photograph: Emmett Jay Scott

Photographs courtesy of Dan Williams

Dedicated to the Memory of Four Remarkable,

Beautiful Baltimoreans:

Sondra Banfield Dailey

Macfarlane Dailey

Michael Sylvester Dailey

Marvin Darrell Dailey

All Taking Langston Hughes' Suggestion to Heart:

"Birthing Is Hard

And Dying Is Mean

So Get Yourself A

Little Loving In Between"

CONTENTS

ACKNOWLEDGMENTS

A number of individuals encouraged and contributed to this primer by sharing their knowledge and expertise. Dan Williams (deceased) archivist of Tuskegee Institute's Hollis Burke Frissell Library was always especially cheerful and helpful in tracking down sources and photographs. Several prominent scholars contributed as editors and/or reviewers in prodding me to rethink certain arguments and claims. I extend my heartfelt appreciation to them: Walter Friedman, professor, Harvard University; Lloyd Hogan, professor, Hamphire College; Ernest Allen, professor, University of Massachusetts—Amherst; James L. Conyers, Jr., professor, University of Houston; Natalie A. Naylor, professor emerita, Hofstra University; Douglas Brinkley, professor, Rice University, and John Allen Gable (deceased) formerly executive director of Theodore Roosevelt Association and adjunct professor, Hofstra University; Bradley R. Rice, professor emeritus, Clayton State University; Alusine Jalloh, professor, University of Texas at Arlington; Toyin Falola, professor, University of Texas at Austin. The author/editor assumes responsibility for any mistakes. Enormous gratitude to Louis Woods, associate professor, Middle Tennesse State University, who read the introduction and made several critical suggestions.

The publisher is thankful for permission to reprint the following copyrighted material.

Maceo Crenshaw Dailey, Jr., "Neither 'Uncle Tom' Nor 'Accommodationist': Booker T. Washington, Emmett Jay Scott, and Constructionalism," Atlanta History: A Journal Of Georgia and The South, Volume XXXVIII, Number 4 (Winter, 1995): 20-33.

Maceo Crenshaw Dailey, Jr., "Bothersome Biography," Black Lives, ed., James L. Conyers Jr., (New York: M. E. Sharpe, 1999): 197-210

Maceo Crenshaw Dailey, Jr., "The Business Life of Emmett Jay Scott," Business History Review 77 (Winter 2003): 667-686.
Maceo Crenshaw Dailey, Jr., "The African Union Company of the 1920s and Its Business Activities in Africa and the United States," Black Business and Economic Power, ed. Alusine Jalloh and Toyin Falola (New York: University of Rochester Press, 2002), 526-538.

Maceo Crenshaw Dailey, Jr., "An Easy Alliance: Theodore Roosevelt and Emmett Jay Scott, 1900-1919," Theodore Roosevelt: Many-Sided American, ed., Natalie A. Naylor, Douglas Brinkley, and John Allen Gable (New York: Heart of the Lakes Publishing, 1992), 471-484.

Maceo Crenshaw Dailey, Jr., "Calvin Coolidge's Afro-American Connection," Contributions in Black Studies, 8 (1986-87): 77-100.

Maceo Crenshaw Dailey, Jr., "Booker T. Washington And The Afro-American Realty Company," The Review of Black Political Economy, Vol. 8, No. 2 (Winter, 1978): 184-201.

INTRODUCTION

The essays herein call for new ways of thinking about and examining the Black leader Emmett Jay Scott within the configuration of the Booker T. Washington movement. Second in command to Booker T. Washington and subsequently an important leader in his own right, Scott served in an almost faultless manner as dedicated loyalist and disciple. An appropriate assessment of his behavior—successes and failures—should make for greater African American headway, where the lessons are heeded, in the great American drama of race which continues to unfold in both splendid and perverse ways. If we malign and continue to play the dozens with the legacy of black leaders such as Scott and pass such musings off as critical reflections, then we continue to flounder and lose ground. Raising serious questions and extracting meaningful lessons must be at the core of studies on African Americans. As the novelist Ralph Ellison presciently warned us many years ago, there are all too many instances of:

> "Prefabricated Negroes ... sketched on sheets of paper
> and superimposed upon the Negro community; then when
> someone thrusts his head through the pages and yells 'watch
> out there Jack, there're people living under here'they are
> shocked and indignant."

Ellison's admonition has always been central to my thinking about the subject matter at hand. In our unhealthy deprecation and suspicion of Scott, Booker T. Washington, and other leaders and followers of this movement, we do not learned much instructively about good old fashioned fundamentals that were at the center of the developmental activities of these individuals. Many were former slaves or individuals only a generation removed from slavery, not afraid of hard work and determined that it should result in better living conditions and opportunities for themselves and their progeny.

In examination of the life of Emmett Jay Scott, I hope to offer motivational insights into the political economy of the Booker T. Washington movement and era in which it flourished. Scott was characterized by one of his contemporaries as the only man who "could walk on snow without leaving footprints," and by another as a "smooth egg." His life was shrouded in secrecy, but enough of his behavior was apparent for the discerning person—contemporary and present day historian---to counter arguments and the many misinterpretations of him and Washington as being mostly myopic and misguided.

In this book's first essay "Neither 'Uncle Tom' Nor 'Accommodationist': Booker T. Washington, Emmett Jay Scott and Constructionalism," the "Uncle Tom" and "Accommodationist" viewspoints are challenged by using the term "Constructionalist," a word Scott and Washington drew on significantly in proselytizing and pontificating.

The second essay in this volume, "Bothersome Biography" focuses on the issue of autobiography (the author's in this case) as a determinate of the kind of biography produced. The essay also points to some of the problems in writing biography, especially within the context of the history and direction of the African American community—viz., what questions are posed, the extent to which the biographer might break with conventional wisdom, and the reluctance (sometimes modesty) in people of color in telling their stories.

The next two essays—"An Easy Alliance: Theodore Roosevelt and Emmett Jay Scott, 1900-1919" and "Calvin Coolidge's Afro-

American Connection"—focus on the political behavior of Scott at two very different times in his life: the first while serving as Booker T. Washington's private secretary and the second when Scott was a leader in his own right in the Republican party and held the position as secretary-treasurer and business manager at Howard University. One finds primarily in Scott a "doer of the deed," and not merely a puppet of the power structure.

The essay "Booker T. Washington and the Afro-American Realty Company," concentrates on the complications emerging when a political and economic partnership is formed within the context of a reform movement. "The Africa Union Company of the 1920s and Its Business Activities in African and the United States," shows Scott ahead of his times in reaching into Africa for economic opportunities beneficial to Africans and African Americans.

The last essay of this volume, "The Business Life of Emmett Jay Scott," reveals the range and reach of Scott's business endeavors.

As Scott aged, he became increasingly aware of detractors and concerned about the legacies of himself and the Booker T. Washington movement, and so in his waning years he carefully crafted his own obituary as a corrective to negative assessments. Nonetheless, he still emerges in the pages of history as a scoundrel or "a crook if ever there was one," in the words of Alain Leroy Locke, the first African American Rhodes Scholar and philosopher. The essays in this book focus on "what do we learn," about the life and legacy of Scott when we divest ourselves of sophistry and drop tendentious name-calling.

NEITHER "UNCLE TOM" NOR "ACCOMMODATIONIST": BOOKER T. WASHINGTON, EMMETT JAY SCOTT, AND CONSTRUCTIONALISM

American historical scholarship did much in the 1960s and 1970s to change the image and conceptualization of Booker T. Washington from "Uncle Tom" to "accommodationist." In either interpretation, however, Washington is viewed as a failed leader. According to Prof. Louis R. Harlan, the Pulitzer Prize-winning biographer and ranking scholar of the "accommodationist school," Washington's "greatest failing" was his inability to "reverse the hard times for blacks during what whites called the Progressive Era." This seems a heavy burden to lay at the feet of one black man without acknowledging the responsibilities of so many other powerful men of the period from 1895 to 1915, most of whom were not black. It is also ironic that in the scholarly debate over whether Booker T. Washington can best be described as an "Uncle Tom" or "accommodationist," little attention has been paid to Washington's own statements about the benefits and value of his leadership approach. In essence, historians and their larger lay audience have neglected to examine Washington on his terms.[1]

This essay takes another look at the Washington movement and its leadership and raises new questions. Were Booker T. Washington and his followers misguided leaders as the "Uncle Tom" and "accommodationist" interpretations suggest? What exactly is meant by the term "accommodationist"? Is there another conceptual means of examining the leadership objectives and behavior of Washington and his followers? Can the Washington movement be studied in a way that takes into account more fully the obstacles Booker T. Washington faced, his time frame for amelioration of racial problems, and his promotion of substantive/infrastructural economic, political, and sociocultural growth and development in the black community?

At the onset, it is important to come to terms with the word, "accommodationist" (since the derivation of "Uncle Tom" is clear to most) and to recognize that the case for labeling Booker T. Washington as such rests on flimsy evidence, unexplained terminology, and the flawed paradigm usage of many of Washington's scholarly critics. In fact, in many ways the writings of professional historians and sociologists who have focused on Washington and his movement reveal more about the peculiar penchant of these scholars to miss obvious lessons, about their myopic viewpoints on racial matters, and their proclivities for hiding behind already established intellectual guidelines than they reveal about Washington himself. These scholars tend to portray Washington and other Black leaders as people primarily acted upon rather than as proactive individuals with their own goals and ideals. On the whole, this kind of history results in a tendency to criticize blacks for failing to take action, while at the same time often denigrating and devaluing most of the actions that they did take. Much of this kind of history writing and analysis is embedded in the term "accommodationist."[2] It is important, therefore, to understand how this particular expression came into being.

The accommodationist label, paradoxically, had its origins on the campus of Tuskegee Institute in Alabama at the time when the Tuskegee principal was being challenged for hegemony in the black community. As Washington witnessed the rise of a formidable group of African American intellectuals, activists, politicians, and a few businessmen challenging his role as leader, at his very feet at Tuskegee sat the budding white sociologist Robert E. Park, who was anxious to serve the school's principal and to understand the ramification of race and class in clearer social science terms. The young scholar, with a recently earned Ph. D. in hand from the University of Heidelberg and heady notions of racial reform, became Washington's traveling secretary on occasional trips between 1908 and 1911. Park also authored several pamphlets and articles that the Tuskegee principal published. It would be Park the scholar who, in embarking upon his formal academic career at the University of Chicago, would try to place the Booker T. Washington movement in some framework that would prove instructive, logical, and perspicacious in understanding race relations.

At times Park exhibited an impish and occasionally sardonic wit when it came to examining race relations. He once wrote, "I am not quite clear in my mind that I am opposed to race riots, the thing that I am opposed to is that the Negro should always lose. If they [blacks] had a fair chance of winning once in a while, I don't know that I would be in favor them [riots]. [3] Park appeared to struggle on more than one occasion for a certain sociological solecism. He argued that the first thing one had to do with a student who wishes to become a sociologist was to show the student that a contribution can be made if he or she does not try to improve anybody. Park also believed that a "moral man cannot be a sociologist."[4]

Despite his protestations about the nature of his discipline, Park was, in fact, a moralist. As he himself later admitted, at the beginning of his professional life he had searched for some great cause or movement to which to attach himself. Park found such a cause during a brief stint of work for the Congo Reform Association that brought him into contact with Tuskegee and Booker T. Washington. Here Park found the opportunity that he desired to explore some of the great moral questions of the day pertaining to race relations. His admiration for Thomas Dewey, one of his teachers, helped to condition his thinking about the connection of scholarship and research to positive social change. Park was, as historian of sociology Fred H. Matthews argues, an idealist who had proclaimed that "the most beautiful thing in life next to love for a woman is to die for an idea in which one believes."[5]

Although Park was dedicated to betterment of humankind, he seldom allowed his students or colleagues to see this side of his intellectual orientation. Instead, he emphasized the importance of scientific inquiry uninfluenced by the practical concerns of society. Park expressed a particular dislike for the saccharine reformers of the "true believer" variety, who, to him, were meddlers, interlopers, and frequently contributors to, rather than alleviators of, social problems. As a result, Park maintained a crusty veneer, which he used to intimidate poor graduate students (including noted black sociologist E. Franklin Frazier) into respect for the discipline of sociology. But despite this outward demeanor, Park sided as an intellectual reformer with the downtrodden, including blacks.

Park believed foremost that blacks had to play within the rules of the society, eventually rising to beat whites at their own game. In this regard, there was much that was Washingtonian in Park's thought. He also believed that people at the bottom, whether they be poor African Americans, Irish, Jews, or Italians, contributed to the vitality and progress of a society in infusing it with their own particular brand of unique characteristics and positive values. Unfortunately this belief in specific characteristics for each ethnic group, while well intentioned, sometimes led Park to some racist conclusions.[6]

"The temperament of the Negro as I conceive it," Park wrote in his collaborative work with Ernest Burgess, *Introduction to the Science of Sociology*, "consists in a few elementary but distinctive characteristics, determined by physical organization and transmitted biologically. These characteristics manifest themselves in a genial, sunny, and social disposition, in an interest and attachment to external, physical things rather than to subjective states and objects of introspection, in a disposition for expression rather than enterprise and action."[7] How Park could hold such a view after his experience at Tuskegee and continue to do so in later years is an enigma that cannot be explained easily. Perhaps, however, the answer can be found partially in the sociologist's own favorite statement by Harvard University philosopher William James, that there is a certain blindness in every human being.[8] In Park's case, this blindness was revealed in his reliance upon the accommodationist framework (that he had helped formulate) to explain the complex process of cultural assimilation and the Negro's place in this process.

In general Park used the accommodationism model to explain the process whereby immigrant and ethnic groups were transformed into Americans by accepting "the social heritage, traditions, sentiment, culture, techniques" of the community and nation in which they lived. By this means, social groups could move toward political, economic, and social empowerment. Park described the process as follows: "The problems of community organization are for the most part problems of accommodation, of articulation of groups within the community and of adjustment of the local community to the life of the wider community of which it is a part...The survival of the organism is based on adaptation and accommodation...adaptation is an effect of competition and accommodation is the result of conflict." Where the Negro fitted in this formulation and sociological model was an important question for Park. He solved the conundrum in the intellectual fashion of the mainstream academic community of his day—i.e., by drawing on decidedly racist thought. It boiled down to sociology about black folks for the intellectual consumption of white folks.[9]

First, Park provided the scholarly audience with a bit of old-fashioned racial stereotyping. In their widely used sociology textbook, Park and Burgess wrote, "The Negro is, by natural disposition, neither an intellectual nor an idealist like the Jew; nor a brooding introspective like the East Indian; nor a pioneer and frontiersman, like the Anglo-Saxon. He is primarily an artist, loving life for its own sake. His *metier* is expression rather than action. He is, so to speak, the lady among the races." The peculiarities of the Negro become secondary to his fate, as Park viewed it. "We are confronted by the obvious fact," Park averred, "as undeniable as it is hard, that the African will only partially assimilate and that he cannot be absorbed. He remains an alien element in the body politics. A foreign substance, he can neither be assimilated nor thrown out." Park and Burgess identified a societal model composed of "conflict groups" and "accommodation groups." Races were classified as conflict groups along with gangs, labor organizations, and nationalities. Accommodationist groups were clubs, social classes, castes, denominations, and nations. The distinctions, needless to say, were not as clearly drawn and precise as one might wish, a problem which was compounded by the many forms of accommodationist behavior that Park himself listed— viz., to the climate, socialization, acceptance of folkways, mores, laws, and customs.[10] It was also unclear, within this context, whether African Americans were to be viewed as a race, caste, or social class.

The sociologist's interpretation of the two great African American leaders of his day—Booker T. Washington and W. E. B. Du Bois— and the difference between their leadership styles and goals are also instructive. Park paid particular attention to the conflict between these two black leaders, and his opinions about these men and their ideas are revealed in the cryptic notes he prepared for lectures to his University of Chicago students. Of Washington, Park wrote, a "mulatto, ugly...traveled with him through Italy, Sicily and people looked at him...thought him so ugly. Washington interested in seeing people trying to find groups further down than the Negro. Had built his own school according to own conceptions. Started in a hen-house. Always reading newspapers. Community really benighted. To North, poor white [.] 'Poor white a good fellow: had his peculiarities, but he can't help it; must just accept him. Had hopes, but treated pragmatically....as a problem."[11]

Park's assessment of Du Bois was more flattering, demonstrating the respect that one scholar might pay to another—at least, as much as racism would permit in that particular era. He thought Du Bois "handsome, graceful, aristocratic in every case except toward opponents...showed toward them no graciousness...carried self with considerable superiority; felt both negroes and poorer whites to be very inferior. Always clever, trying to upset someone else with his argument....Grew up among well bred people. Every opportunity for school. 'spoiled boy' from the first. Early developed an inferiority complex....Scholar, poet. Idealist a flight from reality."[12]

Comparing the two individuals directly, Park concluded that "Washington was orientated in his world. Du Bois always afraid to meet people[.] Can't expect poets to deal with mobs....Critical, unforgiving. Expected Angle-Saxon to be superhuman. Washington didn't expect so much of white man, and consequently got along well." Another difference between the two men, according to Park, was that Du Bois "appeals to 'rights' in 14th & 15th Amendments. Trying to make these laws which exist operative. Went no further. Emancipation still going on. Washington recognized that right and duty to keep in his place was deep in the mores of the South. Du Bois never realized it. In the whole civilization any law passed did not destroy immediately the mores and those things not discussable. Washington: notion gradually dawned on him that the negro was engaged in a struggle with the 'man lowest down.'...Every immigrant group has same struggle. Our democratic groups have same struggle, and was made through such a struggle. People coming in are regarded as utilities, implements by means of which to carry on the common life. Du Bois torn and tormented by conflicting impulses. Expects white race to be all that God intended. But dreaming that some lovely day black and brown people would be sitting on top of white race and crushing. Fanatical type of mind." Though Park's intellectual formation of the problem of race in American society could be confusing and contained a certain flippancy and some bad sociology, his views were not all bad from the black man's point of view: there was still some vague commitment to social justice.[13]

Parkian thought heavily influenced many historians and other scholars who hastened to appropriate the term "accommodation" to explain questions of race relations. These scholars, however, failed to explain the contextual sense in which they were using the term. In short, "accommodationism" was appropriated and blurred by scholars who apparently never took the time to explore fully what Park had meant originally by the word or to examine the way in which it was being used to explain race relations and leadership issues. This increasing reliance upon the word "accommodationism" to describe and explain Washington and his movement is illustrated in the important works of Gunnar Myrdal, Jack Abramowitz, August Meier, and, most recently, Louis Harlan.[14]

In *An American Dilemma*, his classic work on race relations, Gunnar Myrdal made the earliest and most gallant effort to deal with the term "accommodationism" as a conceptual model for examining Booker T. Washington. "It is wrong to characterize Washington," Myrdal explained, "as an all-out accommodating leader. He never relinquished the right to full equality in all respects as the ultimate goal. But for the time being he was prepared to give up social and political equality."[15] Although Myrdal questioned the wisdom of examining Washington as an "all-out" accommodationist, later historians and sociologists did not generally heed his advice. Furthermore, while Myrdal rightly warned the reader of the intellectual problems inherent in relying on the accommodationist framework, he did not explore more fully Park's definition and use of the term itself.

Coming on the heels of Myrdal and attempting to explain some of the paradox of Booker t. Washington, historian Jack Abramowitz, in his 1950 Columbia University dissertation "Accommodation and Militancy in Negro Life, 1876-1916," argued that African Americans were essentially confronted with choosing between the accommodationist and protest style of leadership. Abramowitz's thesis appears to rest conceptually, for the most part, upon the unpublished manuscripts that Ralph J. Bunche submitted for the Carnegie-Myrdal study published as *An American Dilemma* in 1944. "By accommodation," Abramowitz, wrote, "I imply a willingness to accede to the desires of the dominant white group. This group accepts—directly or tacitly— the belief that the Negro is totally or partially inferior and must be protected against his own follies. Those believing in accommodation would agree that the Negro should either shun politics or accept a minor role in the political affairs of his community and nation. He should also accept the type of education that places emphasis upon manual labor and prepare for work which is presently available in the community in which he lives. Above all he must do nothing that might antagonize the dominant white group for their good will is essential to his future progress."

There is, however, a certain ambiguity in Abramowitz's thinking regarding the accommodationist framework. He conceded that in Booker T. Washington's definition of the "Tuskegee Idea" there were "evidences of incipient Negro nationalist feeling," particularly in terms of Washington's advocacy of "Negroes supporting and patronizing their own people."[16]

Despite acknowledging the "evidence of Negro nationalism [that] the 'Tuskegee Idea' contained," Abramowitz eschewed such an emphasis in favor of the accommodationist model and terminology for his interpretation of Booker T. Washington.[17]

Relying heavily on a simplistic reading of the Bunche-Myrdal-

Abramowitz writings, the historian August Meier, in his otherwise useful discussion of Washington in the book *Negro Thought in America, 1880-1915* also characterized Washington as an "accommodationist," though he never really explained to his reading audience what he meant by the term. (To Meier's credit, however, he used the word "accommodation" with a small letter a, thereby somewhat minimizing the term as an official label.) It is clear, though, that Meier's interpretation drew on the Parkian model. In his bibliographical comments, for example, Meier acknowledged that he made "considerable use" of the "standard sociological and historical works on the American Negro," especially "the Research Memoranda prepared for the Carnegie-Myrdal Study." It is therefore perhaps not surprising that Meier also viewed Washington as an accommodationist. "All in all, in viewing Washington's philosophy," the historian wrote, "one is most impressed by his accommodating approach. By carefully selected ambiguities in language, by mentioning political and civil rights but seldom and then only in tactful and vague terms, he effectively masked the ultimate implications of his philosophy. For this reason his philosophy must be viewed as an accommodating one in the context of Southern race relations."[18]

Meier's book represents an important contribution to the scholarly analysis of Booker T. Washington and the movement that he helped launch. To Meier's credit, he did portray Washington as a practical man of affairs, and much of his account does go beyond the simple accommodationist construct, as when he alludes to Washington's masking of his "ultimate implication."[19] Despite this, Meier's discussion is still flawed by its final characterization of the Tuskegee principal as an accommodationist.

The scholarly discussion of Washington and his historical significance has been continued and expanded by Louis Harlan. In the first of his two-part biography of Washington, Harlan began by wishing that he could place Washington on the psychiatrist couch and use psychoanalysis to uncover the many personalities of this complicated man.[20] In a letter to this author, Harlan acknowledged his conceptual problems in grappling with Washington. Nevertheless, he made it clear that as far as he was concerned, the accommodationist framework, however imperfect, seemed the best explanation of Washington and his activities.[21] Nonetheless, Harlan's work has the same limitation as that of preceding historians and sociologists—i.e., there is no discourse on the prior use of the Parkian term "accommodationist." So while Harlan paints a complex portrait of Washington and the Tuskegee movement, the two became all too mechanistic to fit easily into the scheme of American historical analysis, where there is still some ambivalence about the significance and importance of reform movements led by blacks. The problem with the general analysis of many early white scholars, as novelist Ralph Ellison once observed, is that the scholar appears to be unwilling to raise the pages of information for fear that under them one might find people clamoring for a more thorough account of their history. The result is that "prefabricated Negroes are sketched on sheets of paper and superimposed upon the Negro community; then when someone thrusts his head through the pages and yells 'watch out there Jack, there're people living under here.' They [the scholars] are shocked and indignant.'"[22]

When the pages are raised on the Washingtonian movement, one finds a theme in the Tuskegee endeavors and ideology that even W. E. B. Du Bois was later to concede had some merit. Du Bois, the scholar who thought that America could and must rise to the challenge of democracy, wielded his mighty pen in an attempt to make that possible. His scorn and wrath could shake whites and blacks alike who raise his ire. Ever aware of the country's racial maladies, Du Bois came to believe in the early 1930s that maybe Washington was not all wrong, not all bad. Perhaps the idea of a state within a state, *imperium in imperio*, might do much to ease blacks along the correct political and economic course toward self-help and uplift within their own communities. The American Communist Party, then vying for black members, reached a similar conclusion and urged that African Americans be granted control of five states of contiguous territory in the southern part of the United States. Black people, in effect, were being urged to go it alone, to collect themselves, to determine what they had to do to build organizations and institutions from within and thereby contact communities that held the best promise for their people. There was a Washingtonian streak in all of this, best identified not as "accommodationism" but as "contructionalism," the term that the Tuskegee founder had originated and preferred.[23]

Washington and his closest and most important lieutenant, Emmett Jay Scott, his private secretary from Texas, referred to themselves as "constructionalists." As they saw it, their task as statesmen of the African American community was to construct policies and programs to deal with the imposition and problems of racism, rather than to react with mere words or with the threat of retaliation. Despite this self-identification as "constructionalists," historians and scholars of the man and his movement have so far tended to omit the term in their discussion of the Tuskegee movement. In short, the key question is whether Washington and his disciples can be be understood in terms of "Uncle Tomism," "accommodationism," or "constructionalism."[24]

Washington and his followers, of course, would have recognized and been prepared to deal with what they viewed as the false accusation of "Uncle Tomism." They, however, would not recognize the modern day use of the term "accommodationism," nor would they feel terribly flattered that modern historical discourse has promoted them from "Uncle Toms," to "accommodationists."

Clearly, Washingtonian followers, past and present, would prefer a better image, a more accurate understanding of the Tuskegee movement. The historian is compelled to listen more intently, albeit critically, to the Washingtonians' side of the "story," and at least to allow the historical characters to speak on their own terms. Washingtonians viewed their task as constructing a community and carving out space in a country inclined to keep them at the bottom of the social, political, and economic ladder. The axis on which much of Washingtonian thinking rotated was how best to stimulate institutional and organizational growth and development for black people. The long list of institutions and organizations founded under the Washingtonian movement need not be cited here, nor is this the place to reemphasize the preoccupation with jobs and schools that were at the core of the Tuskegee principal's activities. What is important to understand is what animated Washington and his followers to concentrate in such a manner on these objectives and what ideology sustained them despite the petty bickering in the movement.[25]

As mentioned above, the word that the Tuskegee individuals used to define themselves was "constructionalists." Constructionalism was their religion on earth, allowing them to rise above a certain frustration level to focus on using their energies for task-oriented solutions to problems. When Jesse Thomas, one of Washington's young charges and fundraisers, told the Tuskegee principal that he thought of himself as a beggar when he approached wealthy individuals for Tuskegee contributions, Washington replied that one was a beggar only if one wanted the money for oneself. Requests were noble, indeed necessary, when in the cause of a people and reform. This is what the faithful, true believers in the Washington movement understood: that their accomplishments and efforts had to transcend personal concerns for the most part and that they had to stand outside of their own narrow interest at critical moments. It should be observed, however, that there was some sophistry in Washington's reply to Thomas and much self-interest among many in the Tuskegee movement. Tuskegee loyalists were attempting to survive in what was a dangerous world for blacks, and personal interests conflicted with community orient goals frequently enough to make their actions sometimes contradictory. On the whole, however, Tuskegee followers seemed to have understood that personal achievement, the uplift of the individual, and allegiance to the grand cause were the means of uplifting themselves and the community.[26]

Washington, moreover, understood that change would take time, declaring that "during the next half century and more, my race must continue passing through the severe American crucible." As for his particular role, Washington fervently reminded his critics, "The weakest race or individual can condemn a policy. It is the work of a statesman to construct one." Washington advised constantly that "we need organizations for every walk of life." No years passed at Tuskegee without an intense effort to identify the needs of African Americans and to consider institutional or organizational changes that might bring about some important uplift within the black community. The stories are legendary of black farmers, teachers, preachers, and politicians coming to Tuskegee for official or unofficial meetings. The National Negro Business League was, perhaps, the most significant of all of Washington's organizations, even though it never became self-sufficient.[27]

Scholars generally have tried to have it both ways in their analysis of the Tuskegee movement and its place in the black community. On the one hand, they have criticized the movement for taking little action to ameliorate racial injustice, while on the other hand dismissing as unwise or fruitless most of the programs and directives that were created or endorsed by the Tuskegee leadership. Critics have suggested that the programs of the Tuskegee movement were anchored in wish fulfillment or were based on mythological or misty concepts of racial advancement. The result is that the Tuskegee leadership has been assessed much of the blame for the failure of racial progress in the late nineteenth and early twentieth century. Such critics, in general, have not been too optimistic regarding the capacity of blacks for excellence and achievement.

Other, more perceptive interpretations can be offered to explain what truly was going on during those racially nightmarish days shortly after the turn of the twentieth century. Significant insight can be achieved by examining the activities of Washington followers who remained active in the movement after the death of their leader. In this way, one can see the greater long-term implications of turn-of-the-century strategy and tactics. By considering these implications, one can also better understand why some Washington followers became active in the movement of Marcus Garvey; why a number of the disciples of Washington continued business and political efforts from the 1920s to the 1950s to build and strengthen the black community from within; and how they acted to bring money and direction to educational institutions for the training of black professionals. Who were these individuals, what animated them, what did they do? These are some of the important questions that need to be explored.[28]

Key Washingtonians included T. Thomas Fortune, Wilford Smith, William H. Lewis, Mary Bethune, and Emmett Jay Scott. In addition, there was a host of other individuals who were active on state and local levels. It is impossible in this essay to follow the lives of all such individuals, but it is instructive to examine one extraordinary individual who was very close to Booker T. Washington, his private secretary, Emmett Jay Scott. He was not only the closest person to the Tuskegee principal, but also the individual who outlived almost all of the others who had been personally associated with Washington. By examining Scott's long life, one can better understand the meaning and the tenacity of those in the Tuskegee movement.[29]

Scott traveled from Texas to Tuskegee in 1897 to serve as Washington's private secretary. He had been the key figure in the early 1890s in the establishment of a black newspaper, the *Texas Freeman,* in his hometown of Houston. Also while he was in Texas, Scott worked for Norris Wright Cuney, the South's most powerful black political boss. Thus, Scott had exposure to journalism, business, and politics at a very young age. He enjoyed both the intrigue of politics and the independence that came with entrepreneurial endeavors.

At Tuskegee, Scott, possessing a near photographic memory, was able to rely on his experiences and ability to serve Washington in many ways, supervising the receiving and answering of a plethora of letters, standing in for his boss at important political meetings, overseeing the annual conferences of major organizations such as the National Negro Business League, and slipping the figurative stiletto, when need be, in the backs of Washington opponents. No one was more loyal to Washington or a greater admirer of the Tuskegee principal than Scott.

Having lost in his bid for the Tuskegee principalship when Washington died in 1915, Scott might have been expected to be bitterly resentful since he had invested so much time and energy in the Tuskegee movement. But whatever private disappointment he may have experienced, he clung publicly and tenaciously to the faith as a Bookerite.

In 1917 Scott was appointed assistant on Negro affairs to Secretary of War Newton D. Baker. In this wartime role, he labored to stir black patriotism to a feverish pitch, but he also kept African American abreast of many economic gains that could be made as a result of the war. He urged blacks in the military to purchase insurance contracts that would provide for their families in the tragic event of the soldier's death. Scott also prodded African Americans on the home front to invest in Liberty Bonds for revenue-producing income in the war's aftermath. Leaving the War Department, Scott moved on to assume the position as secretary-treasurer and business manager of Howard University in 1919. There he used his political connections to Republicans to bring about passage of a bill that would guarantee annual federal government funding for the university after 1926.

During the 1920s, Scott was to be found plying politics and trying to make a dollar in business while the black community's attention, at least as modern day historians tend to interpret it, was focused on the Harlem Renaissance and the Marcus Garvey movements. There were, however, other concerns and issues in the black community during the 1920s, and many people carried on in Booker T. Washington fashion by preoccupying themselves with business and jobs that came as a result of independent efforts or political ties.

The Garvey movement, with its similar emphasis on economic independence and jobs, did attract some of Washington's most influential followers (including newspaperman T. Thomas Fortune and attorney Wilford S. Smith), but the Tuskegee Machine as led by Scott during the 1920s guided most of Washington's former lieutenants. Scott and his colleagues centered their efforts on entrepreneurship and political patronage, and much of this carried over into the 1930s, even though the political and economic dislocations of that decade meant loss of party favors and dire difficulty in promoting the concept of black capitalism.

Scott's most significant contribution to the economics of African American uplift following Washington's death came during World War II. This advancement, however, was achieved within the restrictive framework of racial separation. Blacks, so long barred from segments of the labor force and from better-paying jobs, warmly welcomed the issuance of President Franklin D. Roosevelt's Executive Order 8802, which required that African Americans make up at least 10 percent of the labor force of firms receiving government contracts. Philadelphia magnate John Pew, owner of the Sun Ship Building Company, complied with the broad spirit of Executive Order 8802 by hiring blacks but placed them in a separate yard. To run the yard, Pew hired Scott and his own handpicked management crew and equipped the black-run yard with modern technology to enhance productivity.

Though the National Association for the Advancement of Colored People (NAACP) condemned the experiment and the National Urban League remained equivocal about it (withholding open criticism largely because of support for Scott), there were several things about the arrangement that augured well for black American laborers. Upper level management was all black, and down through the ranks African Americans also were given secondary and tertiary supervisory positions. The yard employed some ten thousand blacks, including some released from jail, during the height of its busy four-year schedule of shipbuilding. Black women, who were also employed at the Pew yard, set records for labor productivity.

Pew also called upon Scott to increase black participation in the local Republican Party—a somewhat ironic assignment since it was FDR, a Democratic president, who had helped create these wartime jobs for blacks. Scott, a longtime Republican, obliged. Unfortunately, with the end of the war, Black workers who had obtained skills through training programs in the yard were soon released to face a more competitive and less artificial postwar job market.

This thumbnail sketch of Emmett Jay Scott's activities gives a glimpse into the realm of what Scott referred to as "constructionalist" endeavors. This "constructionalist" interpretation of Washington and the movement he launched was also emphasized in a book that Scott wrote on his boss and mentor entitled *Booker T. Washington: Builder of a Civilization* (Garden City: The Country Life Press, 1916). The book conveyed what Washington and Scott wanted others to understand about the Tuskegee movement and its followers—that they were attempting to build a civilization within the black community. In the mid 1940s, Scott reintroduced the theme for a younger generation in an essay written for the *Pittsburgh Courier*. "If Tuskegee were to succeed and the Tuskegee idea to be extended," Scott declared," [then]... Washington, Scott, Logan, Taylor, and others too numerous to mention...[had to foster] under their magic formula, not only Negro education, but Negro journalism, Negro business, Negro fraternal, the Negro church, and the Negro professional classes."[30]

On another occasion when Scott was asked to address the question of black leadership, he wrote to H. J. Mason, publicity officer of Wiley College in Marshall, Texas. "It seems to me that, at this time more than ever, we need a sane, well balanced leadership untainted by personal agitative rhapsody. In other words, the problems ahead of us are practical problems and they can only be solved, if they are to remain permanently settled, by a long range vision....As you know, for many years, I have generally been regarded as a conservative radical or as a radical conservative. If you followed my articles in the press during the past 3 years, I do not believe you will note a single instance in which I compromise any fundamental principle affecting the race....At the same time, I have not failed to recognize the fact that to carry out the purposes we have in mind, it is necessary to do so by a firm insistence upon fundamentals. Frontal attacks have not, in the past, got us very far along the lines of achievement."[31]

Notwithstanding the fact that Scott was obviously defending himself, his focus on that "firm insistence upon fundamentals" was in essence a consistent characteristic of his leadership career and the foundation of his constructionalism. Scott's life and career were dedicated to constructing a policy that promised to move, or as it frequently appeared to many of his contemporaries and critics, to inch blacks along the lines of economic, political, social, and educational gains. To concentrate on this in the analysis of Scott and to see his life as an extension of the career of Booker T. Washington is to tell a story more complete and significant than the prevailing accommodationist framework of interpretation. More importantly, the constructionalist approach offers the promise of a new historical interpretation with more relevance and appeal to black Americans who are coming to see with each new succeeding generation the complications of their history and to understand, as Ralph Ellison explained, that a people cannot survive merely by reacting.[32] Planning, projecting, and providing were the critical concerns for those in the Tuskegee movement as the Washingtonian legacy should reveal.

As this essay has shown, most of the scholars who have examined the Washingtonian movement during the last seventy years have overlooked or ignored the constructionalist theme and its short- and long-term implications for the African American community. Benjamin Brawley, the early black Atlanta historian from Morehouse College, however, recognized and acknowledged the significant achievements of Booker T. Washington and his disciples. "The twenty years from 1895 to 1915," Brawley wrote in his book *A Social History of the American Negro*, "formed a period of unrest and violence, but also of solid economic and social progress, the dominant influence being the work of Booker T. Washington." This is the history of Booker T. Washington that we need to study in 1995 to construct ways of dealing with the internecine conflict and intra-violence in today's black community, and to promote "solid economic and social progress" in the interest of African Americans and the nation at large.[33]

(Endnotes)

1   August Meier, Negro Thought in America, 1880-1915: Racial Ideologies in the Age of Booker T. Washington (Ann Arbor: University of Michigan Press, 1968) Louis R. Harlan, Booker T. Washington, The Wizard of Tuskegee, 1901-1915 (New York: Oxford University Press, 1983), preface, viii.

2   Robert E. Park and Ernest Burgess, Introduction to the Science of Sociology (Chicago: University of Chicago Press, 1969); Jack Abramowitz, "Accommodation and Militancy in Negro Life, 1876-1916," Ph. D. thesis, Columbia University, 1950; Meier, Negro Thought in America; Harlan, Booker T. Washington.

3   Winifred Raushenbush, Robert T. Park: A Biography of a Sociologist (Durham: Duke University Press, 1979), 12-120; 97 for quotation; Fred H. Matthews, Quest for an American Sociology: R. E. Park and the Chicago School(Montreal: McGill-Queen University Press, 1977), 7-168, 189.

4   Raushenbush, Park, 97.

5   Matthews, Quest, 14.

6   This interpretation is based on a synthesis of information drawn from Raushenbush, Park, and Matthews.

7   Park and Burgess, Introduction to the Science of Sociology, 138-39.

8   Matthews, Quest, 32.

9   The quotation is from Park and Burgess, Introduction to the Science of Sociology, 138-39, 663-65, 718-21, 760; for the rest of information in paragraph see Lewis A. Coser, Masters of Sociological Thought (New York: Harcourt Brace Jovanovich, Inc., 1977), 320-21, 351, 357-84. Park acknowledged that the term "accommodation" was initially employed by James Mark Baldwin, a late nineteenth century social psychologist.

10 Park and Burgess, Introduction to the Science of Sociology, 138-39.

11 See Robert E. Park, "Lecture Notes for Course, 'The Negro in America, University of Chicago, Spring, 1931,'"30-35, Robert E. Park Papers, box 1, folder 15, University of Chicago Library, Chicago, Illinois.

12 Ibid.

13 Park, "Lecture Notes for Course," 30-35.

14 Gunnar Myrdal, An American Dilemma: The Negro Problem and Modern Democracy, 2 vols. (New York: Harper and Row, 1944), 739; and the above mentioned works by Meier, Abramowitz, and Harlan.

15 Myrdal, American Dilemma, 739.

16 The Tuskegee idea, according to Booker T. Washington, stressed that "correct education begins at the bottom and expands naturally as the necessities of the people expand. As the race grows in knowledge, experience, culture, taste, and wealth, its wants are bound to become more and more diverse; and to satisfy these wants there will be gradually developed without our own ranks...a constantly increasing variety of professional and businessmen and women. Their places in the economic world will be assured and their prosperity guaranteed...for about them will have been established the solid bulwark of an industrial mass to which they may safely look for support....in this cumulative way there will be erected by the Negro, and for the Negro a complete and indestructible civilization that will be respected by all whose respect is worth the having." Abramowitz, "Accommodation and Militancy," 186.

17 Ibid., 186, 241.

18 Meier, Negro Thought in America, 110,281.

19 Ibid., 85-121, 207-56.

20 Harlan, Booker T. Washington, vii.

21 Louis R. Harlan to Maceo Crenshaw Dailey, Jr., Nov. 10,1984; letter in the collection of the author of this essay.

22 Ralph Ellison, Shadow and Act (New York: Random House, 1953), 123.

23 Herbert Aptheker, The Correspondence of W. E. B. Du Bois, vol. I, selections, 1877-1934 (Amherst: University of Massachusetts Press, 1973), 420-21; E. Davidson Washington, Selected Speeches of Booker T. Washington (New York: Doubleday, Doran, and Co., 1932).

24 For the fullest discussion of Emmett Jay Scott's life and career and the term "constructionalism," see Maceo Crenshaw Dailey, Jr.'s "Emmett Jay Scott: The Career of a Secondary Black Leader," Ph.D. thesis, Howard University, 1983.

25 For this interpretation, I rely heavily on my dissertation and the fourteen edited volumes of Booker T. Washington Papers (Urbana: University of Illinois Press, 1972-84), commendably assembled by Louis R. Harlan and coeditors.

26 See, for example, the standard works by August Meier, Negro Thought; and Louis R. Harlan, Booker T. Washington, The Making of a Negro of a Negro Leader, 1855-1901 and Booker T. Washington: The Wizard of Tuskegee, 1901-1915; Jesse O. Thomas, My Story in Black and White (New York: Exposition Press, 1967), 70-71.

27 Washington, The Speeches of Booker T. Washington, 52, 77, 97, 255; Dailey, "Emmett Jay Scott," 1-197".

28 See Louis R. Harlan's fourteen volumes of Booker T. Washington letters and papers; Tony Martin, Race First, The Ideological and Organizational Struggles of Marcus Garvey and the Universal Negro Improvement Association (Westport, Conn: Greenwood Press, 1976), 56.

29 The following discussion is drawn from Dailey, "Emmett Jay Scott," passim.

30 See Scott's essay for *Pittsburgh Courier*, box 67, Emmett Jay Scott Papers, Morgan State University, Baltimore, Maryland. I am uncertain whether the essay was published. A check of the *Pittsburgh Courier* did not result in locating the published essay, so it may have remained unpublished.

31 E. J. Scott to H. J. Mason, Sept. 21, 1942, box 63, Emmett Jay Scott Papers, Morgan State University.

32 Ellison, Shadow and Act, 315-16.

33 Benjamin Brawley, A Social History of the American Negro (1921; reprint, New York: AMS Press, 1971), 373

BOTHERSOME BIOGRAPHY

A set of complex and compelling forces prompted me to select Emmett Jay Scott, Booker T. Washington's legendary private secretary, as my dissertation biography topic at Howard University in 1975. Malcolm X's statement "that of all our research history is best suited to reward all endeavors" was the reason I indeed remained at Howard University to struggle with the biography on Scott, enduring even arrest after my one-person protest demonstration in the president's office. A student of the remarkable 1960s, caught in the vortex of change and continuity of the 1970s, I had turned Malcolm's statement into a preoccupation with biography to shake the tree of history for intellectual, developmental, and personal fruit.[1]

I wanted to understand, through the life of Emmett Jay Scott, Booker T. Washington and his movement, from the vantage point of my own frustrations with the 1960s and the fears of the 1970s. I was convinced that a moment of progress in one era was being turned into a mountain of problems in the other with the collapse of the Civil Rights Movement; with the deaths of the Kennedys, Malcolm X, Martin Luther King, and Medgar Evers; with the flight from the country of Stokely Carmichael; with the incarceration of H. Rap Brown and Angela Davis; with the fizz-out of the student movements (white and black); with the election of Richard Nixon and Watergate. The velocity of historic change was leaving me feeling disappointed with the pace of progress for African Americans, and biography turned, amidst these circumstances, into a search for meaning and alternatives. History hinged, in my youthful mind, on helping people through the maze of Americanism and difficulties they faced, and I anxiously accepted the challenge of bothersome biography in focusing on the long and productive life of Emmett Jay Scott.[2]

There were the *four* quaint ditty phrases echoing in my mind as I
began my research--ones I recalled having heard as child and young
adult as the "dozens" (i.e., artistic craftsmanship of trivia joke
swapping) were played by African American historians, intellectuals,
activists, and others, caught in the throes of struggle and the horns
of dilemmas:

"NAACP stands for The National Association For Certain People"
"UNIA stands for the Ugliest Negro In America who was
Marcus Garvey"
"A black communist is an overeducated West Indian"
"B.T. in Washington's name stands for 'Bad Taste'"

It was the last charge with which I grappled in my examination
of Booker T. Washington, Tuskegee Institute, and the Tuskegee
Movement. The approach would be in studying the secondary and
tertiary individuals in the Booker T. Washington movement, to raise
questions related to their gravitation to the great African American
leader, the nature of their involvement and support, and their
endeavors in the aftermath of Washington's death in 1915.[3]

Emmett Jay Scott was an easy choice, though I had to expend
enormous intellectual energy getting acceptance for the fact that
he was worthy of a dissertation. This difficulty, though seeming at
one point insurmountable, was mild compared to the problem of
constructing Scott's life once I went to examine the primary data.
There were the myriad private letters in the Booker T. Washington
Collection reposed in the Library of Congress, the two hundred
boxes of Emmett Jay Scott Papers housed at Morgan State University,
the numerous secondary sources of newspapers, magazines, and
pamphlets, and the increasing volumes of biographies and other
scholarly syntheses on the subject of Washington and ancillary

issues. These made my task indeed a daunting one. I sought quick solutions as I importuned my Ph.D. advisor, Dr. Arnold Taylor, to let me do a limited version of Scott's life for a quick exit with full credentials from the graduate school: a political biography or a first-part biography covering the first half of Scott's life. He, however, was a staunch believer that Howard University indeed had to live up to its reputation as the "capstone of Negro education," as well as of African American elevation, so I received a resounding no to all of my proposed intellectual panaceas for a prematurely awarded Ph.D. I learned one valuable lesson that I quickly impose upon my students anxious to write biography as a means of understanding the past and other possibilities: if you must write the biography, pick someone who made a few profound contributions and had the good sense and grace to die young. Emmett Jay Scott did not accommodate me in either of these regards. He lived to the age of eighty-four and did so much and embarked on so many varied activities that one wonders that he had not found his way into print much earlier in a biography- no matter how inchoate or however much based on secondary sources or hearsay. So I went to work on his life, trying to unravel the many mysteries.[4]

My quest was to be as imaginative in my biographical construction as my mentor and history professor Dr. Benjamin Quarles had been in his opening lines of his Frederick Douglass biography, where he wrote, "Douglass seemed to be a man destined for the pulpit or platform, six feet tall and a baritone voice.'[5] I had a similar pithy, if harsher, statement on Scott, given to me by former Howard University historian Dr. Charles Wesley and archivist Dorothy Porter as I dined with them one evening in Washington, D.C.: "Scott was the *only* man who could walk on snow without leaving footprints." This presaged my exploration into the life of an African American who was neither fully hero nor villain, but rather perceived by many contemporaries as a sneaky person, devious in his devotion to Booker T. Washington, and, therefore, too dangerously powerful for a Negro. Setting out to examine Scott's life led me into backwaters and bedrooms to explain the developments of a black community from Reconstruction to the Civil Rights Movement and, more especially, during the Booker T. Washington era and legacy.

I learned foremost, through the life *of* Emmett Jay Scott, what a determined group of African Americans had achieved behind the troubling and now un-American wall of segregation; that separation had compelled African Americans of an earlier era to be straightforward about their difficulties and had fostered a rare brand of dedication, duty, and diplomacy. Scott was the personification of all this. His Houston, Texas, birthplace, where the Klan and other white reactionaries swaggered across the stage of history, was a place where Blacks had found agency (to use the new word in the lexicon of many African American intellectuals) in their resolve to build survival and progressive institutions and organizations. Perhaps *I* was too keenly aware of the accomplishments of black Texans owing to my disappointment with what should have been a better legacy of the Civil Right movement of the 1960s or with what seemed to be lackluster leadership and confusion in the aftermath of Martin Luther King's assassination. As I studied deeper *into* the realities of both periods-Scott's and my own-juxtaposing the two in my mind and not immediately on paper, *I* began to understand the extent to which the African American community was driven by charismatic leadership, and that *if* individuals of the status and ability of the Douglasses, Truths, Tubmans, Booker T. Washingtons, W.E.B. DuBoises Martin Luther Kings, and Malcolm Xs were not on the scene or horizons as prominent national leaders, there stemmed the belief that not much was happening to deal with or ameliorate racial conditions.[6]

I found, however, an interesting pattern, explaining the trajectory of the black community from 1860s to the 1960s. The initial phase and important period of the pattern were the decades between 1865 to 1895, an era of profound organizational and institutional growth and development in the black community. The institutional and organizational developments on the local-community levels gave rise to a remarkable and visible second stage where extraordinary leadership bestrode the black community from 1895 to 1915--essentially the age of Booker T. Washington, lda Wells-Barnett, Anna J. Cooper, Mary Church Terrell, T. Thomas Fortune, and W.E.B. DuBois, who were preoccupied with institutional and organizational structures for African American progress. With the formation of the NAACP and the National Urban League (NUL), two of the more prominent organizations, came the third stage of organizations and institutions, from 1909 to post- World War II. Out of this came the fourth period of leadership of the Civil Rights Movement, from 1945 to 1968; Martin Luther King Jr., and the array of black students emanating from African American colleges of the South. In alternating and symbiotic periods (one age fueling the other) of heightened activities by institutions and organizations, followed by stunning leadership personalities, I found the problematic pattern of progress for the black community. When strong, powerful black leaders were not found on the national level, the historian's gaze was best directed to the local black communities, where local leaders were subsumed by and functioned primarily within organizations and institutions. They may not have been as strong or charismatic as those rising to national fame and prominence, but they were in the trenches, inching the black community along the way to reform and development by their emphasis on institutions and organizations and poised to attach themselves at some point to stronger black leaders on the national level--should such individuals appear. More than likely, those local institutions and organizations (where leaders of lesser ability were to be found) proved to be training, ethos-instilling grounds for leaders of the next stage.[7]

Hence the importance of Scott, a product of the local institutional and organizational developments in the small enclave of Houston's black community and his being propelled out of such a neighborhood and era to hitch his wagon to the Booker T. Washington glory train. Scott understood so well what Washington was trying to achieve, owing to his experiences in Houston. He had pulled himself up from poverty through family, church, and community, all part of the institutional and organizational structures and the chorus of commitment and creativity that were dealing with the race question. He attended college, started a newspaper, and earned the reportage title of "Get Together Scott" for his editorials exhorting Blacks to unity. The lesson here was a simple one that explained Booker T. Washington's "cast down your buckets" and "separate as the fingers of hand"-shibboleths as the progressive views of black leadership, not conciliation and compromise.[8]

Booker T. Washington's popularity in the black community and his sudden rise were explained to me through the prism of Scott's life as an important by-product of the cadre of African American local leaders who saw and heard in the Tuskegee principal's platform and plans many ideas consistent with their own as they sought to build and strengthen institutions and organizations in their hamlets, neighborhoods, towns, cities, and states. They were driven almost to obsession with this, and saw a means of elevating their struggle *to* a national level, a national movement in the persona of Booker T. Washington. Where two or more met and identified a problem, there were later inchoate rumblings of movement-in Florida, Mississippi Alabama, Texas, Georgia, North and South Carolina, Tennessee, and Maryland. These were the troubled states of the South, where they had been so 'buked and scorned." Their heroes and heroines were people of dignity and of so much culture that they became the "Black Bourgeoisie" to white and black scholars and people trying to conceptualize and understand them. Those African Americans of the late nineteenth century had come to know their Plato and Bach in their preoccupation with African American talent and competency. They too were building a civilization: Afro-Saxons, perhaps, but riveting in its purpose and charged with the concept, as the black theologian Alexander Crummell stated most challengingly: "You have got to organize a people who have been living nigh two .hundred years under a system of the most destructive mental, moral, and physical disorganization the world has ever seen." Against this backdrop I began to understand the black men and women of the nineteenth century: their determination, exuberance, and quest for excellence in forging the field, factory, and flower of life into a flotilla of advancement for black folk Their lives when captured in prose almost had the power to burn the pages as we read of African Americans distancing themselves from slavery, moving through segregation, and shaping the society of the future. How was all of this possible, I merely had to look at the life of Scott at Tuskegee.[9]

Emmett Jay Scott, who lived from 1873 to 1957, maintained an almost impossible regimen of work as be labored incessantly and indefatigably to sustain Booker T. Washington. Responding to letters, traveling as emissary, gathering intelligence, signaling out foes to be dealt with, encouraging Booker T. Washington in moments of lull and loss, Scott somehow managed, along with his wife Eleanora (nee Baker) Scott, to keep his family intact and on line for progress. The five Scott children were well trained; two attended elite white colleges and became part of the "Talented Tenth," which black scholar W.E.B. DuBois saw as the salvation of the black race. Scott also succeeded in writing four books, numerous essays, and newspaper articles; enjoying a brief affair with Alice Dunbar Nelson; going to Liberia to try to save the country from financial ruin; and carrying on the feud with W.E.B. DuBois as they both moved through the first half of the twentieth century. Serving as special assistant on Negro affairs to Secretary of Army Newton D. Baker from 1917 to 1919, as secretary-treasurer/business manager of Howard University from 1919 to 1932, and as secretary of the institution until 1938, and moviemaker, adviser to Republican Party until the early 1950s, and investor in business ventures in both white and black communities, Scott was a man of many talents and was involved in numerous activities for the promotion of African Americans and his own self-aggrandizement. He seemed blessed with a blissful marriage, although on at least one occasion he did break his vows of loyalty to his much esteemed and admired wife Eleanora, who died in 1939. His wife's death brought closure to the larger and most significant phase of Emmett Jay Scott's life.[10]

Scott himself died a man of achievements and distinction in the late 1950s, though his death went mostly unnoticed by African Americans. He was clearly another conundrum in the historical interpretations of the Booker T. Washington movement. His life reveals in many ways the often quoted phrase by the savant Santayana that those unaware of their history are doomed to repeat it. In the instance of African Americans, however, ignorance of history meant being locked in a time warp without either a past or future possibilities. A significant African American reading of Booker T. Washington and his movement, instead of confusion and scholarly name—calling, might have placed Blacks in a better position to make meaning and promise of their status as American citizens. In this sense, the nervousness that others shared about the importance of Scott as a biographical subject seemed very misguided. His life opened for me many fascinating vistas of African American history and consciousness. To read about the machinations of those at Tuskegee Institute as they sought to wend their way through the complications of life in the deep South and maintain their professional demeanor was intriguing indeed.[11]

To explore subsequently Scott and a similar group of African American politicians, educators, and activists in the Washington, D.C.— then believed to be the "Black Man's Paradise" —offered another extraordinary profile. Certainly there was the element of plebeian and bourgeoisie synthesis in Scott's life. He was not the one-gullah black Southerner recognizable to most who know the history of Booker T. Washington; nor was Scott comfortable in the DuBoisian camp of northern African Americans, those formally educated Blacks arrogantly aware of their abilities. Scott was, however, a bridge between the two factions, working for Booker T. Washington, but yearning for the sophisticated company, status, and breeding of New England-trained black intellectuals. At Tuskegee Institute, he walked and worked among farmers and persons of "practical affairs." At Howard University, he sought to be a force sustaining the great Negro university as that universal educational point of piety and progress in the black community.[12] Neither plodder nor intellectual, Scott was, however, a striver with a modest but important record of achievements among activists, business individuals, and intellectuals alike. The great Howard University biologist Ernest Just is reported, in his request for funds for a culture of amoebae, to have received a Scott reply that the campus could not have the species "swarming like a herd of elephants." It is unlikely that Scott did not know of amoebae; it is more probable that he meant it as a joke, if indeed the quote is really his. Scott was clear about having at Howard the kind of faculty it ultimately came to have in the brilliant cadre of scholars of the 1930s and 1940s. He merely thought that they should all be Republicans and submissive before administrators-an impossibility even given the marginal job opportunities for black scholars at a university constantly struggling for funds and resources. Scott spent the waning days of his life and career in a remarkable job as director of the Sun Shipbuilding Yard Number 4, where he showed the prescience and organizational skills that could only come, perhaps, from someone steeped in the ideological movement and behavior of Booker T. Washington, where the emphasis was on getting things done. In a shipbuilding yard that employed 10,000 African Americans at the height of its productivity, where a ship per month was completed and christened, Scott was scarred by his Washingtonian willingness to accept a segregated yard and labor experiment, despite the fact that his creditable claim of paying jobs, incomes, and opportunities outweighed apartheid at that moment in the employment sector. People without work and jobs and still in the throes of the Depression were being called upon then by the NAACP to bank on integration in the long run. This seemed risky business and not much consolation to the starving and unemployed.[13]

Scott's personal experiences in Chester, Pennsylvania, would have consequences evident in the Black Power movement and the Black Panther Party of the late 1960s and mid 1970s. Scott's son Horace, a physician and philanderer, fathered a child out of wedlock. The child, Elaine Brown, would later become consort to Huey P. Newton, provisional head of the Black Panther Party, and author of her own remarkable autobiography *A Taste For Power*. Elaine used her grandfather's legacy and life as one of the builders of Howard University in a futile attempt to prod school administrators there to allow Huey Newton to speak on campus. The set of Scott genes are evident in the remarkable resemblance Elaine bears to her grandfather and her stunning capacity for recall, redolent of

Scott's ability for memorization of details. Elaine's writing of her autobiography gave her a fuller appreciation of the importance of her grandfather's life, and she contacted me about certain phases of his career. She too was convinced that Emmett Jay Scott had marched shrewdly through the black community and rightly deserved a biographer. I, of course, marveled how Scott had managed well to hide his tracks frequently, embellish his reputation for public consumption, and add to the enigma of Washingtonian legacy.[14]

Biographical methodologies, paradigms, and theoretical perspectives were important to me as I tried to construct Scott's life, testing approaches of other scholars and reviewing what should be central issues in the examination of an individual's story. The requirements of narrative prevailed in just trying to follow Scott in his footsteps through the late nineteenth and first half of the twentieth century, and in using, as one attendee at Professor Kenneth Silverman's monthly New York University evening seminar and dinner affair (for those, scholars and lay persons, in the city working as biographers) cautioned me, "just good old-fashioned good sense and judgment."[15]

My choices of graduate schools were clearly the best selections for me. Enrolling in the history department master's program of Morgan State University, I had the good fortunate to work with some of the greatest minds anywhere in academe: white or black, the United States or the world. The great Benjamin Quarles was there, and his classes were inspiring and informative. Another faculty member was the young David L. Lewis, who was bringing closure to his biography on Martin Luther King Jr., and would go on to a stellar career, garnering most recently a Pulitzer Prize for his biography of W.E.B. Du Bois. There also was Robert Johnson, a University of Wisconsin Ph.D. and brilliant lecturer in the classroom, who kept his students on the edges of their seats as he spoke with what seemed to be intimate knowledge of the follies and greatness of historical characters from Tudor and Stuart England. Roland McConnell could bedevil graduate students with his insistence for mastery of the skills of the historical craft, but he gave one a clear sense of the pedestrian demands of the profession. All of these individuals knew their history, but they also knew Negro America and understood that learning, laughter, love, lasciviousness, lechery, liberation, liability, and loss constituted the drama and dialogue of the human experience, and that African Americans did not have to make mystical cases for their successes or shortcomings because they, after all, were members of the human community.[16]

My Morgan mentors were not prepared to exempt Blacks from culpability or creativity by making some special or convoluted case for the specificity of African Americans. They understood that there were special instances of strategy, but the concluding sentences of their lectures and books centered on the issues of the human race. It gave the Morgan scholars their greatness and their capacity for motivation. Their students went forth with no special beliefs that they were better or worse than others, but they knew they had to take the journey of life and redeem themselves before their teachers, preachers, and parents who had carefully nurtured them. If there was any mysticism at Morgan, it was not rooted in any believed essentials of "blackness"—that would make for a lot of madness— but rather in a belief in testing the human spirit and capacity for achievement in spite of disadvantages. This concept drove me to Howard and later to the biography of Emmett Jay Scott. Benjamin Quarles was another reason I attend Howard University; he was insistent that it was the place for me given my interests. He frequently laughed at the many times our paths crossed in libraries in Baltimore and Washington, D.C.; some years later, when he had occasion to write a recommendation for me, he advised that I was a young scholar "who knew where the bodies were buried." Prior to enrolling in the Washington, D.C., fine institution of higher learning, I had taken only minor interest in the fact that Emmett Jay Scott had bequeathed his personal papers, letters, and books to Morgan State University, but at Howard University, I soon had many occasions to return to Morgan State to complete my dissertation biography and talk with a masterful biographer in the person of Benjamin Quarles.[17]

I could not have had a more intense learning experience than as a Ph.D. candidate at Howard University, thanks to the preceding, 1960s-generation of "Negro transformed into black student," who changed the institution so remarkably in those eventful years from 1967 to 1968. Writer Paula Giddings had it right when she observed of her student days there that "you walked into the Administration building, the switchboard now is taken over by students and was running much more efficiently than it ever had before." The students barged into poor Dean Snowden's office, and —in the words of one of them, Tony Gittens— the scholar and administrator "was quite shocked. He was absolutely shocked. He was shaking, he was trembling. And then we just told him that his time had come." When I got to Howard University as a graduate student in 1971, the administration had regained control, and the first words we were greeted with were "never would another class like those students of the 1960s be let into Howard because they damn near tore the university down." We were hardly encouraged by what they thought of us as students, but I believe we brought as much intellectual pressure to bear on our mentors as university student activists of ·the 1960s had in direct confrontation: James Early, Bernice Reagan, Rosalyn Terborg-Penn, Sharon Harley, Evelyn Brooks Higginbotham, and Gerald Gill, to name a few who have made their marks.[18]

Seeking a topic for the dissertation while completing my course requirements for admission to Ph.D. candidacy, I saw the remaining greatness of the Howard University of the 1930s and 1940s and the transformations of the 1960s that went to the core of African American achievement, sustaining an institution whose name was virtually synonymous with concerns for American democracy and commitment to racial reform. The names of Howard University faculty members of that era constituted the who's who of savants. Their body of literature and scholarship still remains mostly unsurpassed in understanding of race, class, and gender in America: Ralph Bunche, E. Franklin Frazier, Ernest Just, Charles Thompson, Rayford Logan, Sterling Brown, Arthur Davis, Dorothy Porter, and Doxey Wilkerson were indicative of those notables at the university. I had the great pleasure of studying with Professors Arthur Davis and Rayford Logan, interviewing Mordecai Johnson, Charles Wesley, Dorothy Porter, May Miller Sullivan, Charles Thompson, and Doxey Wilkerson. They gave me clues, gossips, and facts about Howard University and what they thought of Emmett Jay Scott. They essentially sensitized and frightened me with the difficulty of my task; they sent me forth with the view that I had no other choice but to do my best.[19]

I think in some instances they must have laughed and admired my youthful zeal and perhaps foolishness in trying to tackle, as a graduate student, such a complex, awesome, colossal, and difficult project as a biography of Emmett Jay Scott. Indeed, in some of my interviews, especially the one with Charles Thompson, I was the one essentially interviewed, and he at one point asked me directly what led me to believe that I had the ability to bring the biography to closure with the appropriate scholarly cogency. Professor Thompson had spent many summers trying to make sense of the Booker T. Washington movement and legacy. In the early 1930s, he had complained to Emmett Jay Scott, then at Howard University as secretary-treasurer and business manager, of the difficulty of gathering all the information at Tuskegee and giving it some order for better understanding of that era. His unpublished manuscript has still not been turned into a book, so Professor Thompson was not too optimistic about my succeeding with the Scott biography.[20]

What Howard University and Morgan State University provided for me were laboratories for grappling with African American personalities and individuals who studied or were a part of the struggle for advancement, as well as a glimpse of the lives of individuals who were a part of the great dramas in the black community. I had occasion to talk *with* individuals at those institutions who knew the greatness and follies of many of those remarkable scholars and professors at the African American colleges. While seeking to gather data on Scott and writing the biography, I felt privileged by that exposure and excited by the contacts my education was providing. I was a member of the black educational community and functioning within a compressed and intensive segment of a larger environment and world that I was desperately seeking to make sense of. I was in the crucible. I had presumed to study Scott's life at the same time that it impacted upon my life as an African American and graduate student. I had the opportunity to experience an historical continuum and to interact and interview many of the characters that connected one era to another. Sent from Howard University for oral interviews, I traveled to the North Carolina Mutual Insurance Company in Durham for a meeting with its president; to Atlanta, Georgia, for discussion with Morehouse College president emeritus Benjamin E. Mays and Emmett Jay Scott's sister (who ordered me from her home five minutes into the interview); and to Houston, Texas, to see other Scott family members. Crystallizing in my mind was the fact that my research agenda was beginning to parallel my life, and the biography was beginning to consume me to the extent that my wife and children began to speak of the fact that I was working on the life of "Uncle Emmett," when I could not be found or was off on a research junket. My more cruel detractors were questioning whether I would bring the biography to completeness, either as dissertation or book.[21]

Aware of such cruelties, I resorted to reflections on the childishness and instances of professorial pubescence I have witnessed or heard mentioned in the university: from seeing one scholar chase another around the speaker's platform, to hearing of another rebuke his audience of harsh critics with the retort "your mama," to reading a statement of Congresswoman Shirley Chisolm remarking that she had never understood how vicious politics could be until she taught in college. These thoughts amused me and made me forget outside distractions. I adopted the philosophy of my friend, jazz saxophonist and artist Marion Brown, who once stated, "As long as I know what I am doing, I am cool." Yet for all the travail and the occasional conviction that one is in a profession that comes all too close to pugilistic threats to underscore the validity of scholarly points, still one cannot find a more rewarding form of employment. The crude part of the profession, of course, is the quest for publication. Here politics can surface in the most cruel and disconcerting ways---most graduate schools should actually offer courses in navigating one's early professional path to publication and tenure: a "how to do it" course. I could have profited from such a course.[22]

My biography was submitted to the University of North Carolina Press in the 1980s. I received telephone information and confirmation that the press's in-house review had produced an extremely favorable assessment and that the manuscript would be forwarded to only one reader for comments and criticisms. This small thing seemed all that was required, given the evidence of several statements vouching for the quality of the manuscript and the importance of it for publication. The follow-up response was a devastating one for me, and maybe a blessing in its resounding *no*. The anonymous critic/reviewer was alluded to as someone too powerful to offend or not heed the judgment of. There was no need, so I was told by the letter of refusal, to question the "accommodationist" stance used to interpret the Booker T. Washington movement or the activities of his followers and subordinates. I resolved to return to the biographical drawing board and produce a work that no one could refuse. This, of course, was a mistake. The best strategy would have been to mail the manuscript to multiple publishers, finding one courageous enough and determined to work with me to produce the best possible rendition of Scott's life. I am not too disappointed in my decision at that moment and have been glad that I have done more homework on Scott's life. I shall be mailing the manuscript to potential publishers at the end of this summer. One needs to know when to release a project. If it is, as one pundit put it, a monstrous thing to try to write a biography about someone you have never known and with whom you have never lived, it perhaps is a worse sin not to know when to release the subject from your scholarly grip and into the world, casting it off, so to speak, for it to sink or swim.[23]

Bothersome biography, to say the least, led to a beleaguered scholarly life and an odyssey for me in my determination to comprehend, actively and intellectually, the great American racial drama. Many rewarding moments of my life have been spent struggling with the enigmas of Mr. Emmett Jay Scott. The window of his life opened a verdant pasture to the promises and problems of the black community. Later teaching stints in the North and South gave me first-hand exposure to the worlds in which W.E.B. DuBois,

Booker T. Washington, Mary Church Terrell, Anna J. Cooper, and Emmett Jay Scott inhabited, seeing there the remnants and sometimes casualties of great struggles and the ashes of what could have been a more important legacy. I learned, most significantly, that at the level of life as an African American there were many great examples of honor, decency, and brilliance in the black community and that all of this had to be turned into building blocks. I learned of the extraordinary work ethic of a preceding generation of black giants in social movements and scholasticism; I learned of the cruel mangling of bright blacks too sensitive to survive their critics, white and black; I learned foremost that we could do much better than the spate of leaders guiding us post-1968 and that there were still great questions needing to be addressed under the rubric of race. I learned also that in writing biography, one is writing, to a great measure, autobiography: problems and promises of your own life that you may project on historical characters. This is a good thing, though you should not be surprised if the answers do not come forth readily and with crystal-clear meaning. For me, the central question has been what does it really mean to be black in America, and I sought to resolve that in examining Scott's life. The revelations, the ride, and the rewards have been well worth the wait at the publication gate.

(Endnotes)

1   See Malcolm, X, "On Afro-American History." Unable to pay my student bill at the end of the semester, I was barred from having my transcript mailed to the SUNY Brockport's African and African American Studies Program, where I was being considered for a one-year appointment. After a day of tossing myself on the mercy of Howard University administrators and pointing out that the policy for withholding of transcripts had been rescinded, my frustration, probably owing to the Washington, D.C., heat and humidity, prompted me to march into the president's office with an ultimatum that "'they would have to mail my transcript or arrest me." A faculty trustee, Professor Harold O. Lewis, was kind enough to extricate me from the city police retention center and, strangely enough, I, from this rash act, endeared myself to some of the old-guard faculty members, who admired my moxie.

2   Having lived through the sixties, I strangely have to rely on my notes when I endeavor to teach that period. It gives much credence to Arthur Schlesinger's thesis of the impact of the velocity of history

on the human organism. I am still awaiting the cogent ground-level book that will really capture the essence of that era: its music, poetry, politics, and possibilities. *Eyes on the Prize* is indeed a good effort, bur one comes away from the book and videos believing that "something else," as Ornette Coleman would have it, needs to be said.

3   My schooling in Baltimore with the great "griot" Mary Carter Smith was my introduction to Africa. My elementary school teacher, Mrs. Carter Smith made trips to Africa in the 1950s and returned to educate us about the realities of the continent. She wore clothing and jewelry from Africa, and we students were stunned by her beauty and eloquence. She was walking "Afrocentricity" in the 1950s. Many of my professors, friends, and activists would regale us with these little ditties. Community pundits and preachers also added to the folklore, and Howard University and Morgan State University continued the learning experience of what was said from the "down and under."

4   Maceo Crenshaw Dailey Jr., "Emmett Jay Scott: The Career of a Secondary Black Leader," Ph.D. diss., Howard University, 1983.; see also the works of Professor Louis R. Harlan on Booker T. Washington: *Booker T. Washington: The Wizard of Tuskegee, 1901-1915* (New York: Oxford University Press, 1983); *Booker T. Washington: The Making of a Black Leader. 1856-1901* (New York: Oxford University Press, 1972); and *Booker T. Washington Papers* (Urbana: University of Illinois Press, 1972).

5   Benjamin Quarles, *Frederick Douglass* (Englewood Cliffs, NJ: Prentice Hall, 1968); interview with Charles Wesley and Dorothy Porter, 14 October 1977, Washington, D.C.

6   See Dailey, "Emmett Jay Scott," for this discussion.

7   Ibid

8   Ibid.

9   Ibid.; see also Wilson Moses, *The Golden Age of Black Nationalism* (New York: Oxford University Press, 1988); Benjamin Brawley, *The Negro Genius* (New York: Biblo and Tannen, 1966), 105

10   Dailey, "Emmett Jay Scott."

11   Ibid.

12   Ibid.

13   Ibid.; Kenneth Manning, *Black Apollo of Science: The Life of Everett Ernest Just* (New York: Oxford University Press, 1983), 225.

14   Elaine Brown, *A Taste for Power* (New York: Pantheon Books, !992), *50-55*; 284-85; Dailey, "Emmett Jay Scott."

15   I had a one-semester appointment at New York University, and there had the opportunity to participate in the extremely rewarding evenings in the seminars and in Village restaurants, where we continued our discussions on many evenings. Professor Silverman was a jolly fellow in organizing and guiding us to think more critically about biography.

16   This information is based, of course, on recollections of my graduate career.

17   Benjamin Quarles to Robert Hill, 8 August 1980. A copy of this letter is in possession of the author of this paper.

18   Henry Hampston and Steve Fayer, *Voice of Freedom: An Oral History of the Civil Rights Movement from me 1950s through the 1980s.* (New York: Bantam Books, 1990), 424-49.

19   See Rayford W. Logan, *Howard University: The First Hundred Years* (New York: New York University Press, 1969) for the best synthesis on the richness and importance of the university. My dissertation footnotes cover the many interviews, *so I shall only list a few* places, dates, and names here: interview with Arthur P. Davis, Washington, D.C., 2 August 1978; telephone interview with Mordecai Johnson, Washington, D.C., 21 July 1975; interview with Charles Wesley and Dorothy Porter, Washington, D.C., 14 October 1977; interview with Rayford Logan, Washington, D.C., 2 April 1975.

20   Interview with Dr. Charles Thompson, Silver Springs, Maryland, summer 1977.

21   Dailey, "Emmett Jay Scott," 1-10; interview with Benjamin Mays, Atlanta, Georgia, 27 July 1977.

22   My attendance at various scholarly conferences has led to some experiences that give credence indeed to the thin line between love and hate, and sanity and insanity. People who use words and thoughts to do in their foes are often more cruel and surgical than those who use the rapier. A colleague once left a session where he was discussing his research and remarked joyfully to me that no one in the room had "laid a glove on me." This, needless to say, was a learning experience for me, for I had not yet developed the requisite mentality for survival in the academy.

23   Anonymous reviewer to Iris Tillman Hill, editor-in-chief of the University of North Carolina Press, 1 October 1985. A copy of the letter is in the collection of the author of this essay.

Emmett Jay Scott

Booker T. Washington

Tuskegee Institute: Booker T. Washington in the center of the first row; Emmett Jay Scott immediately to the left of Washington

Emmett Jay Scott, standing on the ground on the left; Booker T. Washington, standing on the top step of the train

Booker T. Washington seated in the foreground of the photograph

Booker T. Washington and Emmett Jay Scott standing next to each other on the second row.

Booker T. Washington at the podium and Emmett Jay Scott immediately behind him at Tuskegee Institute's 25th anniversary celebration.

Annual Meeting of the National Negro Bankers Association in the 1930s. C.C. Spaulding of North Carolina Mutual the third person from left on the first row. The National Negro Bankers Association was an outgrowth of the kind of organizations Washington and Scott promoted for African American uplift.

Vice-President Calvin Coolidge, fourth from the right on the first row and Principal Robert R. Moton standing next to him, along with other luminaries, at dedication of the Veterans Hospital in Tuskegee.

Theodore Roosevelt and Booker T. Washington (center) viewing a parade on the ocassion of Tuskegee Institute's 25th anniversary celebration.

Emmett Jay Scott (the extreme rear) and Principal Robert Russa Moton (right side of photograph) with the white philanthropists and donors visiting Tuskegee Institute.

Howard University's Board of Trustees in 1914, a few years after Emmett Jay Scott retired from the University after feuding with its President Mordecai Johnson who is in front row (fourth from the right).

Mordecai Johnson, who became the first full time African American President of Howard University in 1926. Emmett Jay Scott led the behind-the-scenes campaign to install Johnson as President of the University.

Tuskegee faculty

AN EASY ALLIANCE: THEODORE ROOSEVELT
AND EMMETT JAY SCOTT, 1900-1919

If Theodore Roosevelt, as his son observed, coveted adulation so much that at funerals he desired to be the corpse and at weddings he wanted to be the bride, at least one significant African-American of the twentieth century truly lamented the fact that the "Rough Rider" got his wish in 1919 in regard to one of the choices. Roosevelt, in his political ambition, had not always been kind to that African-American, Emmett Jay Scott, but the black man who had served as Booker T. Washington's private secretary from 1897 to 1912 and official secretary of Tuskegee Institute from 1912 to 1919 was a forgiving individual. He, in fact, had remained more loyal to Roosevelt than any African-American of the twentieth century. The nature of the relationship between Emmett Jay Scott and Theodore Roosevelt, which began in 1897 and continued through to 1919, was filled with promises and paradoxes. It was an easy, almost natural, alliance between two men radically different in demeanor. It was also a relationship couched in mutual respect and admiration, as much as race etiquettes of the time would permit. The illumination of that relationship tells us much about the intersection of education and politics, where racial considerations were fundamental preoccupations affecting choices, and what things were possible in the modern America of the twentieth century. The relationship is also another example of the means by which the twenty-sixth president made an indelible mark on modern America insofar as political choices had to be made in the realm of race relations.[1]

Theodore Roosevelt, a man of inordinate verve, had many things to ponder as he boarded the train for Booker T. Washington's Tuskegee Institute in Alabama the second week in December 1915. Paramount, of course, was Roosevelt's intended bid for the

Republican party's presidential nomination in 1916. In travelling to Tuskegee as one of the most influential trustees of the school, Roosevelt had a chance to strengthen his political hand among African-Americans whom he had alienated earlier in the Brownsville decision to punish black soldiers for the sortie on that Texas town in 1906, and in 1912 when he booted black Republicans out of the Bull Moose convention. In order for Roosevelt to win the good will of the black community for another presidential bid in 1916, it was decided that TR would install in the Tuskegee principalship an African-American leader capable of the political wizardry of Booker T. Washington, the recently deceased black leader who had done so much to tie black Republicans to the chief executive and the Grand Old Party from 1901 to 1909.[2]

Roosevelt had decided that to accomplish his political aim, the vacuum in black leadership and the Tuskegee principalship had to be filled in the wake of Booker T. Washington's death by his alter ego and former private secretary, Emmett Jay Scott. Roosevelt's decision, regarding this matter, was based on a meeting with Washington's ranking New York political lieutenant, Charles W. Anderson, himself a close friend and ally of Scott. Even without Anderson's prodding, Roosevelt probably would have supported Scott for the position. Still lingering in Roosevelt's memory were the frequent and successful meetings with Scott, who was dispatched often to the White House to do Washington's bidding or to provide information on Republican party politics in the South in the years between 1901 and 1909. It appears that the first meeting between Roosevelt and Scott may have occurred, however, as early as 1897 when Roosevelt was undersecretary of the Navy and Scott was then busy adjusting to his new job at Tuskegee. The president developed an abiding respect for Scott's ability, his *savoir faire* and astute political judgment. Their meetings crossed racial and class boundaries-owing to the president's appreciation for intelligence, shrewdness, and style. And why not? Scott, as the black historian Carter G. Woodson once observed, was the "only man who could walk on snow without leaving footprints." A quick recounting of the careers of the two men provides some clues about the easy alliance between them and the importance of this relationship with respect to politics and education in the coming of age of modern America.[3]

Wealth and sickness through the formative years had given Theodore Roosevelt a keen patrician sense of the uses to which power could be put, as well as an appreciation for the underdog. Born in Houston, Texas in 1873, Emmett Jay Scott was the proverbial underdog in the American society. Racial restrictions and violence in the South made the life of most African-Americans extremely precarious. Whereas Roosevelt had the privileges of money and Harvard to see him through the formative years, Scott faced deprivation. An exceptionally bright young lad, Scott did well in the all-black school system of Houston. He attended Wiley College for a few years, but was forced to withdraw ultimately to help sustain his parents in the rearing of their eight children. While Roosevelt was making his initial intrusions into the realm of politics in New York City, Scott was struggling for means to support himself and assist his family.

He resolved the employment matter temporarily by working for the *Houston Post* in the early 1890s, and gained the confidence and courage there to embark upon the task of founding, along with two other individuals in his hometown in 1893, an African-American newspaper titled the *Texas Freeman*. While Roosevelt was realizing his political ambitions on the state level, Scott was hitching his political fortunes to local black Republicans in Texas. Through his newspaper articles and editorials urging blacks to "get together,"

Scott was invited to become private secretary to the state's most powerful black Republican party boss, Norris Wright Cuney. While Roosevelt moved through the Navy Department with his profound appreciation for the theories of Alfred T. Mahan and then headed for the Spanish-American Civil War to don his Brooks Brothers military suit before the charge up San Juan Hill, Scott was searching for other outlets for his talent, which he resolved by accepting the job as private secretary to Booker T. Washington.

The first meeting of Roosevelt and Scott, if indeed it did come in 1897, found both men in the ascendancy of their careers. Scott, as Washington's private secretary, had been dispatched to the District of Columbia to talk with government officials about preventing the encroachment of European powers on the tiny West African Republic of Liberia, the country the United States had helped to establish in the 1830s as a place for the repatriation of former slaves from the United States. Scott, it appears, ended up in a meeting with Theodore Roosevelt, who promised that he would try to seek some assistance for the West African country. The Spanish-American War, however, proved to be the little skirmish that, in part, diverted Roosevelt's attention from the woes of Liberia.[4]

The fame Roosevelt garnered in the Spanish-American War and his placement as the vice presidential candidate on the Republican party ticket in 1900 led to a necessary, but distant familiarity, with black politicians. The vice president, however, soon came to take a particularly keen interest in black politics as practiced by Booker T. Washington. Roosevelt's ambition, and his belief that he could win the presidency in his own right post-1900, led to attempts to strengthen his ties with Washington and Tuskegee even before the assassination of William McKinley. The assassination, in fact, prevented Roosevelt from keeping a date with Booker T. Washington in which the two had planned to discuss Republican party politics in the South. There can be no doubt that Roosevelt intended to make a strong political ally of Washington, and thereby strengthen his hand in the bid for the presidential office when the time came. It was an alliance to which both Washington and his private secretary Emmett Jay Scott looked forward, anticipating the consolidation of their influence and greater control of patronage positions to be allocated to blacks.[5]

All of this eventually came to pass when Roosevelt assumed the presidency in 1901. During his tenure in office, there developed the Tuskegee political machine which Washington and Scott directed in boss-like fashion from the small Alabama black school. Scott himself made numerous trips to the White House to discuss with Roosevelt the political climate in the South, African-American patronage jobs, and black problems Washington thought wise for the president to discuss from time to time. Washington and Scott, owing to this contact with the president, promptly lined up behind his choice of Taft for the presidential nomination in 1908 and supported the next chief executive during his four-year stint in office. In 1912, however, despite Scott's anxiousness to support Roosevelt for the nomination, Booker T. Washington decided to back discreetly the incumbent Taft prior to the nomination contest itself and openly after the matter was settled. As for Roosevelt during that time of frustration, he blamed blacks, in part, for his loss of the regular Republican party nomination and, therefore, barred them from the Bull Moose convention.

To mend political fences all around in the quest for the presidential nomination four years later in 1916, in both the black and white political communities, was a tall order. Roosevelt, however, sought such an opportunity to make amends with

African-Americans in the events following the death of Booker T. Washington. His trip to Tuskegee in late 1915 was motivated by this desire. To draw on the Tuskegee political alliance that had served him so well in 1904 and 1908, Roosevelt turned to Scott, not only Washington's main political lieutenant, but a person whose knowledge of Southern politics was unsurpassed. To some individuals, Scott, indeed, was the brains of the Tuskegee political machine, and this is no doubt what Charles W. Anderson, the black political boss in New York, had assured Roosevelt would be the case in the years after Washington's death. Boarding the New York train for Alabama and Tuskegee, Roosevelt planned consequently to use his power and influence as a trustee of the school to make Scott the principal and heir-apparent to the deceased black leader Washington. Roosevelt was convinced that Scott was the man to galvanize black Republicans and revitalize the Tuskegee political machine, and the former president had hoped to rely on this to win votes and support of African-Americans in his bid for the White House in 1916.[6]

Tuskegee would be no easy place for Roosevelt to work his serious brand of political magic in getting Scott installed as the next principal of the school. Factionalism had already developed at the institution as individuals discussed and sometimes openly stated their preference for the next principal. On the campus, the names of three Tuskegee employees emerged as favorites: Emmett Jay Scott, Booker T. Washington's brother John, and Warren Logan, the school treasurer. Robert R. Moton, employed in Booker T. Washington's alma mater, Hampton Institute in Virginia, was also receiving support for the post. Moton's claim to the post was strengthened considerably by the belief that Booker T. Washington, prior to his death, had endorsed Moton for the principalship. Yet, Booker T. Washington's wife, Margaret Murray, voiced her support for Scott for the position during the initial days of the discussion over a successor. She subsequently changed her mind, however, informing trustee William G. Willcox that the appointment of either of the two men who then appeared to be the primary candidates, Scott, the school's secretary, or Logan, the Tuskegee treasurer, as principal, "would split the campus wide open."

As the decision became more crucial, there emerged unusual timidity and a foreboding mood on the campus over the succession question for two significant reasons: no one wanted to commit openly and thereby run the risk of becoming expendable for supporting the wrong candidate, and most recognized that the decision rested in the hands of the prominent and powerful white board of trustees. Among the most vocal and determined board members was Theodore Roosevelt, who proclaimed that the "President of Tuskegee should be ... the leader of his race in this country"; Sears-Roebuck magnate Julius Rosenwald, who argued that the next head of the institute should be "looked upon as a leader by the Southern white and black people"; and William G. Willcox, who held that the next principal had to "carry sufficient weight ... at the school and throughout the country.[7]

To make the decision regarding the successor, board of trustee members arriving on campus were afforded both social and educational opportunities to get to know better some of the candidates. Particular exercises of this nature were the scheduled ceremonial speeches in memory of the deceased Booker T. Washington. These were the so-called "maiden speeches," to see if the potential candidates had the savvy and political ability to satisfy blacks in the audience with a commitment to racial reform, while not alienating whites with brashness. The scheduling of Warren Logan to speak during the visit of the trustees was such an occasion.

Unfortunately, Logan's wife committed suicide during this period, leaping-from the academic building in rather dramatic fashion as student cadets were marching past the structure. The grief-stricken Logan was excused from the memorial exercises for Washington, and Emmett Jay Scott became the substitute speaker.[8]

Scott was basically a backroom political operator and smooth negotiator. On the public podium, his style was formal and stiff, and justly perceived at times as pedantic and pretentious to the hostile critic. He seldom erred in political judgment, but made a serious mistake in his commemorative speech ·on Booker T. Washington by characterizing him as the man who had laid the economic and political foundation for black uplift and suggesting that the time was ripe to move past 1915 more steadfastly and boldly in the acquisition of all citizenship rights. Addressing the audience and standing with board of trustee members seated behind him on the stage, Scott, in the process of speaking, did not realize the extent to which he had alienated one of his major supporters, Theodore Roosevelt. The former president, perturbed and disgruntled by Scott's presentation, turned to Julius Rosenwald to proclaim that "we can never make this man president because he will not be able to get along with the white folks."[9]

Theodore Roosevelt promptly reversed himself on the Scott appointment for principal of the school. In the first board of trustee session on December 13 (when the group was deadlocked on the choice of Scott or Robert Russa Moton from Hampton), Roosevelt led the movement for establishing a subcommittee of five to determine who should be the next head of Tuskegee Institute. Neither Roosevelt nor Rosenwald, still a firm Scott supporter, served on the committee, but there was no doubt that it was established to represent the two varying views of the two men.

Rosenwald remained committed to Scott as the "one man [who] has sat at the feet of the master and imbibed his spirit, and in addition has the necessary intellectual qualities which the other [Moton] lacks." Roosevelt, however, was prone to reject this argument. On the return trip to New York, Roosevelt convinced several of the board members on his train to invite Moton to join their party on the segment of the journey from Richmond to Washington, D. C. Moton did so, and impressed all in the group, especially Roosevelt. Once in New York, Roosevelt telegrammed Rosenwald that Moton was the man for the job, that he lacked the 'bumptiousness or self-assertiveness which would at once ensure failure in his position." Roosevelt concluded his statement with the observation that he felt "so strongly that in case the committee of Five do not agree [sic] on Major Moton," he would "advise their extending their enquire and looking throughout the Union to find the best man for the position."[10]

A prerequisite qualification for the best man had to be political admiration for Roosevelt. The former president wanted an African-American political ally in the South to marshall votes and support for him. In a Jim Crow society, Moton seemed docile and discrete enough, and able within the African-American community to mobilize black Republicans for the Roosevelt campaign for president. With respect to Scott, it is possible that Roosevelt may have promised him some coveted patronage job in the event the former president succeeded in a third bid for the White House. Rather than harboring disappointment, Scott enthusiastically prepared to galvanize black Republicans for Roosevelt. Scott's cooperation also assured Roosevelt the support of the wealthy Julius Rosenwald whose money and influence would be useful in the Midwest. Thus in that one trip to Tuskegee, Roosevelt had succeeded in many of his political objectives with respect to the African-American community.[11]

Roosevelt, consequently, had much to his political liking within the circle of black Republicans of the South in the initial campaign for the party's nomination in 1916. Scott coordinated the activities of Southern black Republicans in beating the bush for Roosevelt votes. The legendary political supporters of Booker T. Washington and those the Tuskegee principal had been able to deliver to Roosevelt so effectively in the past were all in the field again under Scott's direction, diligently backing the Rough Rider: P.B.S. Pinchback (Louisiana); Charles W. Anderson (New York); Henry M. Minton (Philadelphia); Robert R. Church (Tennessee); Charles Banks (Mississippi); Perry Howard (Mississippi); Ralph Tyler (Ohio); and Walter L. Cohen (Louisiana). Scott came to believe, along with Charles Anderson, that Roosevelt's primary competitor for the presidential nomination was former New York Governor and Supreme Court Justice Charles E. Hughes who, in good conscience, could neither "authorize the use of his name as a candidate with propriety, nor... (that) the convention can afford to nominate him in the absence of such authorization." Scott, however, would see such logic fall prey quickly to the vicissitudes of party wisdom and some unusual political chicanery within his own circle of allies.

One of his closest political allies and lieutenants, James A. Cobb of Washington, D.C., had been duped by long-time Republican politico Frank H. Hitchcock and New York broker Eugene Meyer into accepting money to travel south to uncover as well as build support for Roosevelt. The two white New Yorkers, in reality, were Hughes supporters and wanted to find the extent of Roosevelt's popularity in the South. The duplicity of the two white New Yorkers and the stupidity of his own man Cobb caused some minor annoyance for Scott, but did nothing to deter his thinking that Roosevelt was still a certainty in the nomination contest. All the Tuskegee men further assured Scott that they would follow his lead in the convention and that Roosevelt was their first choice.[12]

The convention proved to be an exciting but disappointing one for Scott. At the conclusion of the convention, Scott felt that he had exhausted himself "putting in some hard licks in behalf of Roosevelt ... hustl[ing] from sun up to midnight." He had indeed worked diligently. At the quadrennial meeting of black Republicans in the famous African-American Episcopal Church of Quinn Chapel in Chicago, Scott coordinated the activities for Roosevelt. African-American Republicans also held several other related activities, in particular a smoker at the Jones Place Restaurant presided over by the notable Chicago black politician Oscar DePriest, all as a part of the numerous social and political events to whip black Republicans into a feverish pitch for Roosevelt. Scott also held some renegade African-American politicians in check. The demands upon the Republican party emanating from this kind of African-American staging and political effort were fairly innocuous, limited primarily to the general but vague political requests of bland planks calling for "Negro Rights" and opposition to any legislation undermining the Fourteenth and Fifteenth Amendments.[13]

Roosevelt's resulting loss of the Republican nomination was, however, a bitter disappointment for Scott, who came to see the convention as nothing more than a "political carnival pulled off" for Hughes. Some of Scott's other political allies at the convention bemoaned similar complaints to him and the fact that Roosevelt's supporters had been caught waiting too late and were therefore outmaneuvered. Walter L. Cohen of New Orleans, long active in Republican party politics, groaned to Scott that it would have been "foolish" to have given delegate votes to Roosevelt on the sixth ballot when it was obvious that the struggle had been lost by that time. Something, however, could be salvaged out of the defeat of Roosevelt. Cohen wrote to Scott that Roosevelt would be wise to give "half-hearted" support to Hughes, anticipate his defeat, and vie for the nomination himself some four years later. Cohen perceptively predicted Roosevelt's tactical approach in the early stages of the presidential race of 1916.[14]

While Scott worked closely with his political ally Charles W. Anderson to get on the inside of the Hughes campaign and control the African-American bureaucracy to elect the Republican presidential nominee, Roosevelt remained aloof of party politics, preferring to retire to Oyster Bay and let the political pundits ponder his next move. Scott enjoyed a modicum of success in establishing himself as a machine-style political boss during the campaign and assisted in swaying African-Americans to support Hughes. He, however, took more than a passing interest in Roosevelt's curious silencing and cloistering of himself in Oyster Bay. Under what probably was Scott's prodding, Charles Anderson visited Roosevelt to discuss the campaign. The black politician left the meeting with Roosevelt convinced, as he later confided to Scott, that Hughes's approach was wrong and that it seemed he was going to lose. Scott was also informed by Anderson of his wish that Roosevelt would rally, stepping in to give Hughes the necessary lift and eventual lead in the race.[15]

With Roosevelt continuing to nurse his bruised ego and the new Republican leaders slow to draw on help from the black community, Hughes's campaign sputtered. In general, the Republican party machinery was lethargic, uninspired, and unorganized. African-American Republicans, under Scott's guidance, were particularly disgruntled; and all seemed rather hopeless for Hughes the candidate-owing to the internecine conflict in the party in both white and black camps alike. The newspapers predicted that Woodrow Wilson's "commanding lead" was too much to overcome. That fall of 1916, however, witnessed a remarkable political blitzkrieg by the Republican party, one that narrowly missed winning the presidential office for Hughes. At the center of this effort were two important individuals: Roosevelt and Scott..[16]

The black Republicans led by Scott launched the "Big Drive." Scott turned to the institutional *black* community that he knew so well, employing the churches, newspapers, black store owners, and especially the barbers and beauticians. The black community became even more caught up in the political fervor as Scott persuaded Hughes to give a speech on the "fundamental rights" of the Negro. Black ministers received a copy of Hughes's "Doctrine of Human Rights," and Charles W. Anderson, Scott's ally, exhorted the preachers to get the black vote out by pontificating on the Sunday prior to the election "that the promise of St. John may be fulfilled that 'ye shall know the truth, and the truth shall make you free.'" Added to all of this was the fact that Roosevelt came out of his exile in Oyster Bay to give a series of forceful speeches for Hughes. The final days of the election campaign led to a significant erosion of Wilson's support among voters, and on November 7, the day of the election, Hughes actually went to sleep believing that he had eked out a narrow victory. Scott thought so too, mailing congratulatory telegrams to that effect to Hughes, Roosevelt, and Charles Anderson. There was, of course, shock for Scott when he realized the following day that Hughes had been defeated, but the black politician did not lament the loss for very long. Travelling to New York City a few days after the election, Scott met with John McGrath, a Roosevelt admirer and backer, to discuss the campaign of the Rough Rider for the presidential nomination and election in 1920.[17]

Scott redoubled his efforts to ensure that he would be in position in 1920 for a strong Roosevelt bid for the presidency by maintaining political ties to blacks and whites to be relied upon at that time. The war years, however, prompted Scott to tum to the more immediate question of the role of African-Americans in the U.S. Army in 1917 and what citizenship gains might be made by blacks owing to their gallant and heroic contributions to the military campaign. As in the past, African-Americans interpreted the war as a chance to demonstrate their patriotism and earn respect that translated into opportunity within the United States. As one African-American wit put it, blacks had to break into each war like burglars, and it was no different during the conflict of 1917.[18]

In the weeks prior to the U.S. declaration of war on Germany in April 1917, Scott drafted a set of resolutions calling for the utilization of African-American manpower and submitted it to Julius Rosenwald, then a member of the National Defense Board. While waiting for the War Department's decision regarding the utilization of black soldiers, Scott travelled to Oyster Bay on April 21, 1917, where he and Roosevelt discussed the formation of an African-American military regiment and appointment of officers the former president planned to take to Europe in the quest for glory. Details of the plan were not found in the papers of Roosevelt or Scott, so it is impossible to uncover the precise thinking of both men with regard to the venture. It is evident, however, that the political capital to be acquired by such an endeavor was the uppermost matter in the minds of both men, and the popularity garnered by such a move would have augured well for Roosevelt in the presidential contest of 1920.

Roosevelt had to bide his time without military recognition, however, and unfortunately, his death some two years later brought an end to one of the most extraordinary political careers in the United States. Scott, during the war, held the highest position accorded an African-American with his appointment as Special Assistant on Negro Affairs to Newton D. Baker, the secretary of the

Army. He later moved to Washington in 1919 to serve as secretary-treasurer and business manager at Howard University. Many years later, during World War II, Scott headed yard number four of the Pew family-owned Sun Shipbuilding Company in Chester, Pennsylvania. Scott remained a lifelong Republican and lived until 1957, the eve of the Civil Rights Movement of the 1960s.

The relationship between Theodore Roosevelt and Emmett Jay Scott had a significant impact on historical development of modern America in the twentieth century. Scott's loss of the Tuskegee principalship propelled him to consider and capitalize on other career opportunities. Tuskegee Institute under Robert Russa Moton stayed within the orbit of the Republican party, with the principal of the school (Roosevelt's choice) remaining all too docile for many African Americans. Roosevelt's calling of Scott to Oyster Bay for the discussion of the role of black troops in World War I was all part of the movement and thinking that military recognition and engagement of African-Americans could be made to serve political ends. White Republicans who began to dominate the party after 1916- with the purge of older politicians such as Roosevelt (who were keener and more sophisticated about relying on blacks and indeed exploiting the black vote)—demonstrated decreasing ability and interest in ways to hold African-Americans in the party of Lincoln. In many ways, it was Roosevelt's patrician sense, ambition, and appreciation for the underdog that allowed him to structure a relationship with an African-American, Scott, that crossed social and racial boundaries. This afforded both men the opportunity to be players, rather than mere passive objects, in the political game of chance and the art of the possible in politics and race relations. Scott, of course, learned what many black politicians of today all too often forget: that ambition and strength among the powerful can be turned to advantages for the powerless with the proper alliances, though individuals are not always guaranteed that personal ambition will be fulfilled.[19]

(Endnotes)

1   John Milton Cooper, Jr., *The Warrior and the Priest: Woodrow Wilson and Theodore Roosevelt* (Cambridge~ Belknap Press of Harvard University Press, 1983), p. 69; Maceo Crenshaw Dailey, Jr., "Emmett Jay Scott: The Career of a Secondary Black Leader," (Ph.D. diss., Howard University, 1983), pp. 236-318.

2   Dailey, "Emmett Jay Scott," p. 189.

3   Ibid., p. 189; John Blum, *The Republican Roosevelt*, (Cambridge: Harvard University Press, 1954), p. 127.

4   Dailey, "Emmett Jay Scott," pp. 1-34; this interpretation is also drawn from David McCullough, *Mornings on Horseback*, (New York: Simon and Schuster, 1981).

5   Dailey, "Emmett Jay Scott," pp. 72-73; Theodore Roosevelt to Booker T. Washington, September 14, 1901, Booker T. Washington Papers, Library of Congress, Washington, DC.

6   Dailey, "Emmett Jay Scott," pp. 66-197.

7   Ibid., pp. 187-89.

8   Jessie Thomas, *My Story in Black and White*, (New York: Exposition Pre s, 1967), pp. 53-58.

9   Ibid., pp. 53-58.

10   Ibid., pp. 53-58; "Tuskegee Institute Board of Trustees' Minutes," December 13, 1915, Tuskegee Paper Files, Hollis B. Frissell Library, Tuskegee, AL; *Tuskegee Student*, p. 1, n.d., College Files, Frissell Library, Tuskegee, Ala.; Ernest T. Attwell to Julius Rosenwald, December 15, 1915; Rosenwald to Seth Low, December 16, 1915; Rosenwald to Low, December 16, 1915; Roosevelt to Rosenwald, December 15, 1915, Julius Rosenwald Papers, University of Chicago Library, Chicago, Ill.; Scott to James A. Cobb, December 22, 1915, microfilm reel 203, Theodore Roosevelt Papers, Library of Congress, Washington, DC.

11   Thomas, *My Story In Black and White*, pp. 55- 56; William G. Willcox to Rosenwald, December 23, 1915, Rosenwald Papers.

12   Dailey, "Emmett Jay Scott," pp. 236-41; Charles W. Anderson to Scott, May 4, 1916, cont. 2; Scott to Anderson, May 2, 1916, cont. 2, Emmett Jay Scott Papers, Morgan State University Library, Baltimore, MD.

13   Scott to Robert Russa Moton, June 4, 1916, cont. 11; Scott to Moton, June 16, 1916, cont. 11, Robert Russa Moton Papers, Hollis B. Frissell Library, Tuskegee, AL.

14   Dailey, "Emmett Jay Scott," *pp.* 244-45; Hanes Walton, Jr., *Black Republicans: The Politics of The Black and Tans* (Metuchen, NJ: The Scarecrow Press, 1975), pp.156-57.

15   Dailey, "Emmett jay Scott," pp. 245-53.

16   Ibid., pp. 257-58.

17   Ibid., pp. 258-62; Anderson to Scott, October 23, 1916, cont. 1;Scott to Parsons, October 17, 1916, cont. 10; Anderson to Scott, July 15, 1916, cont. 1; Anderson to Parsons, September 8, 1916, cont. 1, Scott Papers; George H. Mayer, *The Republican Party, 1854-1964,* (New York: Oxford University Press, 1964), PP;,344-47.

18   Dailey, 'Emmett Jay Scott, pp. 259-60, 263-65.

19   Ibid., pp. 2.65-525.

CALVIN COOLIDGE'S AFRO-AMERICAN CONNECTION

In the wake of President Warren G. Harding's death and the entry of Calvin Coolidge in the White House as chief executive in August, 1923, blacks, like the bulk of ordinary white Americans, were uncertain of what to expect. Nonetheless, those close to the prior presidential administration, whether black or white, had clear reason to believe that Coolidge was preeminently qualified to carry on in the fashion of his predecessor. They anticipated his continued implementation of Republican policies in accord with political promises which had led to the party's overwhelming electoral victory in 1920. Indeed, Harding's breaking of tradition to allow his Vice President Coolidge to sit with the presidential cabinet ensured that the new chief executive understood and was prepared administratively to deal with tariff issues, tax reform legislation, measures for the reduction of the public debt, and the host of other political promises Republicans made in 1920. In 1924 Coolidge, however, had to win nomination and election to the office in his own right in order to continue the quest for legislation consonant with the Republican party political mandate received four years earlier.

In one sense, Coolidge's ascendancy to the executive office and his unfolding, staunch campaign for election to the post in 1924 were reminiscent of the political activities of Theodore Roosevelt in 1901. Roosevelt had aggressively demonstrated that an individual in the generally regarded "dead end" political job of vice president could inherit the chief executive post, wrest control of the party from its recognized leaders if need be, and make a gallant and successful bid to become president. Roosevelt became the first vice president to engineer such a feat, and managed to do so on the formation of a strong political coalition that involved both blacks and whites.

Coolidge's task was not unlike that of Roosevelt, though he would have to duplicate such a feat in less than half the time Roosevelt had had at his disposal. Coolidge's assignment, however, was somewhat less difficult owing to his almost total agreement on economic and political principles with his predecessor, Harding. This was part of the attraction of Republicans to Coolidge. If the President had any major problem at all, it centered on possible political complications arising out of the alarming innuendoes concerning the corruption and scandal of the Harding administration. Such rumors had the potential of undermining Coolidge's credibility and bid for the presidency in 1924 by associating him too much with the Harding administration.[1]

Coolidge moved expeditiously and adroitly toward grappling with this problem and achieving his overall goal of election to the presidency. In the process he shrewdly sought political support from both blacks and whites in the South where Republican popularity would almost assuredly bring about national success for the party in 1924. In bidding for the political backing of white southerners, Coolidge appointed C. Bascom Slemp, former congressman from Virginia to the post as White House secretary in 1923, and also made another southerner, Clarence Sherill, his new military aide and superintendent of buildings and grounds in the District of Columbia. In the quest for the presidential nomination in 1924, he realized their value in the effort to obtain additional white southern support as quickly as possible. Slemp, in particular, did prove extremely useful to Coolidge in his bid for the nomination when the white southerner explained to a congressional committee the nature and extent of the Harding administration scandal. He was able to convince the Republican national convention to forego an earlier ruling that would have reduced significantly the number of delegates from Georgia, Mississippi, and South Carolina, states where the incumbent president anticipated major support. Slemp also impressed upon other white southern Republicans the importance of backing Coolidge for the presidential nomination. In bringing Slemp into the White House, Coolidge, in particular, had succeeded in increasing his stature among Southern whites. The President next turned to the Afro-American community, equally zealous in courting an important political friendship.[2]

In seeking the support of Afro-Americans, Coolidge understood the political implication of the demographic shift of some 400,000 to 1,000,000 blacks from the South in the years between 1910 and 1920 (something most white Republicans seemed to be oblivious or unwilling to grasp fully), and therefore appreciated the potential of the black vote in key states. In Coolidge's papers is a memorandum of 9 August 1924 noting the number of Afro-American voters in the "important states" in the West and North. Attracting these Afro-American voters was the challenge for Coolidge, for they had no especial reason to support him. While the appointments of Slemp and Sherill counted as excellent political strategy for gaining white southern support, they were decisions anathema to many blacks who viewed the two men as little more than segregationists and members of the "Lily White" faction. That faction had emerged in the South in the 1890s on the basis of a political program excluding Afro-Americans from participating and exercising influence in Republican party conventions on the local, state, and national levels. The appointments were not encouraging signs to Afro-Americans, then sizing up a Coolidge who indeed had been almost too quiet as Vice President and was still largely unknown to blacks. Upon becoming president in 1923 about the only virtue he had to commend him to blacks was the fact that he came from New England, a region Afro-Americans associated with the Abolitionist movement of the antebellum era and with more liberal attitudes on matters affecting race relations and citizenship rights for blacks at the turn of the twentieth century. Yet New England had instilled in him none of this strong commitment or determination to improving race relations in the country.[3]

There were reasons, however, for Coolidge's lack of interest in critical racial issues of his day. In Vermont where he was born on 4 July 1872, Coolidge, if the written record is correct, had no familiarity with Afro-Americans or the host of problems they faced. His first exposure to blacks came in a limited manner in the early 1890s when he entered Amherst College. Prominent on Amherst's campus in that period was the accomplished Afro-American student athlete, William H. Lewis, who after graduating from that college obtained a law degree from Harvard University and subsequently became a follower of the unusually powerful black leader and principal of Tuskegee Institute, Booker T. Washington. Lewis' athletic exploits while he was in college caught the attention of Coolidge during his school days at Amherst. In October, 1892, the young Calvin, who attended major athletic contests involving college rivalries, wrote to his father that the Harvard football team had trounced soundly its Amherst opponents by a score of 26 to 0 and that a "negro by the name of Lewis" playing "centre rush" led the Cambridge eleven to victory. This was perhaps the only interest Coolidge expressed in an Afro-American, at least while he was a student at Amherst. [4]

In Coolidge's subsequent career as an attorney in Northampton, legislator, and governor in Massachusetts from 1900 to 1920, and early years as the Vice President of the United States, he focused in a nominal and limited way on issues of concern to Afro-Americans. The sum total of his early political efforts on behalf of the black community may have been a ceremonial salute as governor in 1919 welcoming home Massachusetts black soldiers who fought in World War I and his discussion on 27 April 1920 with then Boston attorney William H. Lewis regarding the possibility of forming a machine gun battalion of Afro-American troops in Massachusetts. This latter recommendation Coolidge transmitted to the Secretary of War Newton D. Baker. Coolidge's later years as Vice President, however, did acquaint him with some Afro-American leaders on the national level. He responded positively to a request in 1922 from Emmett Jay Scott, formerly secretary to Booker T. Washington, to recommend a black, Butler Wilson, for a state patronage job in Massachusetts. Coolidge honored this appeal owing largely to the political support he received from Butler as a Massachusetts delegate to the Republican party presidential nominating convention of 1920.[5]

Later as Vice President, Coolidge had a chance to see an important side of black life in the South when he traveled to Tuskegee, Alabama in 1923 to participate in the dedication ceremony for the opening of the Veterans Hospital. There he met Robert Russa Moton, formerly commandant of cadets at Hampton Institute, who succeeded Booker T. Washington as principal of Tuskegee Institute in 1916. Coolidge came to like the Afro-American leader as well as the brand of educational training he espoused at Tuskegee Institute: trades and crafts or the newest techniques in farming, all primarily in the endeavor to prepare blacks for jobs or land ownership. While in the Alabama town, Coolidge, in a prompt show of support for Moton, volunteered to contribute to efforts to increase the endowment funds of Tuskegee Institute and its sister school, Hampton in Virginia. His appreciation of Moton and the difficulties the black leader faced in the South also led to a significant show of support from the White House when the struggle over control of the Veterans Hospital precipitated racial tension in Tuskegee shortly after the medical facilities were opened.[6]

Tuskegee white opposition in 1923 to Afro-American employment in upper echelon jobs in the Veterans Hospital led to a Ku Klux Klan march on the grounds of the facilities to intimidate blacks then working there. In its sortie on the hospital, however, the white supremacist group avoided marching directly on the campus of nearby Tuskegee Institute where many Afro-American farmers and school alumni had stationed themselves to protect Moton, the students, and the institution identified with the venerable Booker T. Washington. In the midst of this tension filled environment Moton, who was confronted with the difficult diplomatic task of maintaining peace as well as obtaining jobs for blacks in the hospital, received extraordinary support from the White House in accomplishing his two objectives.[7]

By 1923 Coolidge, it seems, had come to sympathize with blacks on some problems regarding their plight in the American society, but perhaps more significant was the fact that in this stage of his political career, he had come to understand these issues through contact with Tuskegee individuals such as Moton, Scott, and Lewis. Like their former leader Booker T. Washington, they were individuals who sought to profit by ties to powerful politicians and philanthropists in the North and South. Consequently, they turned to Coolidge with similar thoughts when he became president in 1923. Coolidge's ties to these individuals, coupled with his willingness to meet with other distinguished reform-minded blacks, augured well for the President during his formative months in office and led to a period of good will between him and the overall Afro-American community.[8]

Coolidge welcomed officials of the Negro National Educational Congress to the White House in September, 1923 and listened attentively to their expressions of alarm about the problems of segregation and discrimination within the federal government. In October the President granted an interview to an Afro-American group brought to Washington by William Monroe Trotter, the fiery black editor of the *Boston Guardian*. Trotter had gained much attention at the turn of the twentieth century as a major critic of Booker T. Washington's public program of placing economic development and trade school education ahead of the struggle for Afro-American voting rights and crusade against segregation codes in the country. (Trotter, who seldom minced words, had been so outspoken on a previous trip to the White House almost a decade earlier that then President Woodrow Wilson, peremptorily terminated the meeting. This made it all the more remarkable that another President, Coolidge, would agree to see the Boston editor.) In that meeting Trotter urged the President to continue to assist Moton in his efforts to ensure blacks a central role in policies pertaining to the Veterans Hospital. Trotter also encouraged Coolidge to give strong presidential backing to an anti-lynching bill expected to come before Congress in 1924, and take steps to increase the enrollment of blacks in West Point and the Naval Academy. After the Trotter meeting, the President met another black delegation led to the White House in that same month by the prominent Afro-American attorney form Richmond, Virginia, Giles B. Jackson, who impressed upon Coolidge the need for a Negro Industrial Commission, a proposal expected to be included in the Delaware Congressman Caleb R. Layton's legislative bill to be considered by the House of Representatives that year.[9]

From the President's viewpoint, perhaps the most significant black visitor to the White House in October was Robert Russa Moton, the principal of Tuskegee, who had come to share with Coolidge information on southern political issues affecting the Republican party. The meeting was the result of a letter from Moton to Coolidge several weeks earlier, advising the President to confer with southern politicians Joseph O. Thompson, a white in Alabama, and Robert R. Church, a wealthy black businessman in Tennessee. Both men, as former Booker T. Washington political associates, had acquired an excellent understanding of the Republican party machine in their region. Their advice, Moton believed, would be useful in grappling with the issues of delegate support in the convention and the possible political strength of the party in their states in the election of 1924. Other Tuskegee-oriented political stalwarts attuned to the Booker T. Washington dictates of obtaining patronage positions traveled to the White House in October, the most prominent being Emmett Jay Scott, then secretary-treasurer and business manager of Howard University, James A. Cobb, a law professor at the same institution, and William H. Lewis. They, as a group, promptly suggested to the President the kinds of black political appointments to be made, and even drafted for Coolidge the necessary wording of a policy statement when the time came to announce to newspapers the anticipated patronage jobs to be given to Afro-Americans.[10]

Though Coolidge was drawn politically to the Tuskgegee-oriented faction as a whole, it appeared for the moment in October, 1923 that his doors were open to other significant black leaders of the press, civil rights organizations, educational institutions, and Republican party as well. Thus, despite initial reservations, blacks as a whole were more optimistic as the new administration began to take shape. An indication of their positive attitude toward the President was reflected in the District of Columbia black newspaper, the *Washington Eagle*, which opined that "much significance is attached to the easy access to the White House which colored citizens now enjoy." Coolidge did remain open to visits and discussions with Afro-Americans, and sought their advice on matters of race relations. Any doubts he may have had about what Afro-Americans

wanted politically must have been dispelled by these meetings. In
particular, he received a long detailed memorandum in November
from the head of the Associated Negro Press, Nahum B. Brasher,
who placed his news service at the disposal of the President as he had
done also for Harding. Brascher wrote to Coolidge, summarizing
and confirming that the issues central to Afro-Americans were
policy changes to stop lynchings, segregation in public offices, and
the discrimination policies of the civil service. Brascher also advised
the President to provide more patronage appointments for blacks in
southern states, and increase the number of black representatives in
Republican national conventions. Resolving all of these problems
to the satisfaction of Afro-Americans would have been a difficult
assignment for Coolidge, but he continued to give hope to blacks
that some reform was forthcoming by his willingness to discuss these
matters publicly.[11]

The pinnacle of Afro-American confidence in the new chief
executive came, consequently, shortly after Coolidge gave the annual
presidential address to Congress in November and opened the
segment of this speech on racial reform with the ringing declaration
that under the Constitution, "the rights of colored citizens were as
sacred as those of any other citizen" and that it was "both a public
and private duty to protect these rights." The President went
on to urge the Congress "to exercise all its power of prevention
and punishment against the hideous crime of lynching." He also
acknowledged that money had already been appropriated to give
black Americans vocational training in agriculture, recommended
federal funds for the medical school of the predominantly black
Howard University to contribute to the overall objective of
producing an additional five hundred Afro-American doctors, and
pointed to the need for a biracial industrial committee to facilitate
the adjustment of large numbers of southern blacks migrating to

northern urban centers in search of jobs and all-around better conditions. Concluding the portion of his speech on Afro-Americans, Coolidge did lessen the sting of these remarks to whites by proclaiming that "it was well to recognize that [racial] difficulties are to a large extent local problems which must be worked out by mutual forbearance and human kindness of each community. Such a method gives much more promise of a real remedy than outside interference."[12]

In these succinct but significant statements the President touched upon issues that had long troubled blacks and for which they had sought solutions on many previous occasions. Lynchings had been a perennial problem since the American Civil War. From 1880 to 1920, some 3.112 Afro-Americans had been victims of lynch mobs in the United States, but congressional legislative measures to end this often racially motivated crime had been voted down on five separate occasions prior to 1923. In 1923, the very year in which Congressman Leonidas Dyer's anti-lynching measure was defeated in the United States Senate, a total of twenty-nine Afro-Americans had been hanged by mobs. Anticipating the reintroduction of the Dyer Bill in Congress in 1924, Coolidge took a courageous step in urging Capitol Hill legislators to pass the anti-lynching measure. The chief executive's recommendation for a biracial commission for easing the settlement of southern black migrants in northern industrialized areas amounted to an endorsement of the Layton bill, one of the goals of which was to facilitate the transition of workers to life in urban regions. This particular bill was scheduled to come before Congress in 1924. Coolidge's pledging of funds to Howard University, an institution experiencing the kind of growth and development in the 1920s which caused blacks to label it "the Capstone of Negro Education," proved extremely soothing to many Afro-Americans who looked to the Washington D.C., center of learning for the much needed cadre of well trained doctors, dentists, lawyers, engineers, preachers, and teachers vital to the welfare of the black community. In all, the Afro-American segment of the President's annual speech before Congress in 1923 was favorably received by blacks who interpreted it as the beginning of new executive sensitivity to assist them in their endeavors to improve their status in the American society.[13]

In the wake of his speech to Congress, Coolidge continued to welcome blacks to the White House and to discuss racial reform issues with them. In February, 1924, the National Association for the Advancement of Colored People led a coalition of black church groups and lay organizations to the White House to discuss varying issues of concerns to Afro-Americans. Within the group were such Afro-American notables as the organization's executive secretary, James Weldon Johnson; the head of its Washington, D.C. branch, Archibald Grimke; president of the Brotherhood of Sleeping Car Porters, A. Philip Randolph; editors Robert Abbott of the *Chicago Defender*; Robert L. Vann of the *Pittsburgh Courier*; and Carl Murphy of the *Baltimore Afro-American*. During the course of the meeting, this group handed to Coolidge a petition of 124,000 signatures urging a pardon for the Afro-American soldiers involved in the racial melee in Houston, Texas in 1917 where 17 whites were killed, a request the President granted a few years later.[14]

Between 1923 and 1924 the alacrity which Coolidge demonstrated in meeting with Afro-Americans proved encouraging to most of them, save for the seasoned and cautious veterans of civil rights organizations and more radical activists in the quest of racial reform. Chandler Owen and A. Philip Randolph, the two brilliant editors of the radical black journal, *The Messenger*, had expressed their apprehension earlier by pointing out that "Coolidge [was] pretty cool on the Negro question." Following his own meeting with the President, James W. Johnson commented some years later that "It was clear Mr. Coolidge knew absolutely nothing about colored people. I gathered that the only living Negro he had heard anything about was Major [Robert Russa] Moton. I was relieved when the audience was over, and I suppose Mr. Coolidge was too." Given the provincial background of Coolidge and his political predilections for Tuskegee-oriented black leaders, Johnson's comments were essentially correct. More critically, they revealed what would become grave and inherent problems in the President's style of leadership: meeting with major representatives of the Afro-American community but ultimately coming to rely on the advice of the "old guard" black politicians. In an era where growing reform organizations and movements heightened the expectations of blacks for positive change, such a strategy made them more impatient with a Republican party which showed less concern with their problems and correspondingly took their vote for granted.[15]

Neither Coolidge nor the Republican party could afford to remain impervious to the growing importance and thrust of black movements and organizations---particularly the NAACP, the unfolding of the "New Negro" artistic flowering known as the Harlem Renaissance centered in upper Manhattan (a place many Afro-Americans believed to be the cultural and political capital of the black community), and the extraordinary mass movement of blacks led dramatically by the Universal Negro Improvement Association and its inimitable, Jamaican-born leader, Marcus Garvey, who immigrated to the United States in 1916. These movements and organizations exemplified the intensity of concern over racial problems and changing emphasis of blacks in the 1920s, and their determination to bring about much needed elevation in the status of Afro-Americans in the United States. Though these three movements were centered in New York City for the most part their tentacles reached significantly into many Afro-American communities in the country and influenced black thought and behavior.[16]

The incipient nationalism of the Marcus Garvey-led UNIA instilled self pride in many blacks and stimulated them to become involved in self-help economic projects on a level more grandiose, though less substantial, than Booker T. Washington, whose program of self-help organizational and institutional development within the black community appeared to be fundamentally applicable to Jamaican conditions. Entering the country after the death of Washington, Garvey, nonetheless, continued with his original plans of involving himself in organizational endeavors for black progress and did his leadership homework accordingly. Garvey traveled throughout the United States between 1916 and 1919 to gauge the plight of black Americans. Settling later in Harlem, he formed the Universal Negro Improvement Association and African Communities League to organize blacks around the world to improve their status. The Association's paramilitary group, capitalist projects, and mass meetings inspired blacks to concentrate on rising above their second-class citizenship in the United States or their colonial status in countries in the Caribbean or Africa. The UNIA's Slogan, "one God, one Aim, one Destiny," soon appealed to numerous blacks in the United States. Perhaps as many as 400,000 individuals joined or supported Garvey and the UNIA during the 1920s. G. Emonei Carter, the first Vice President of the organization, who earlier had served as a waiter in a Florida Hotel Coolidge frequented on vacation, wrote to the President in the manner befitting a proud, racially conscious representative of an organization to the head of a sovereign state, alerting him to the significance of the UNIA. There is no evidence, however, that

Coolidge responded. Garvey and Garveyism were too far outside of the mainstream of American life, and already under the scrutiny of United States military officials and later the Bureau of Investigation for "fomenting" racial hatred. In a curious twist, though, Garvey and many UNIA followers politically supported Coolidge in the 1924 presidential election. But they would voice no similar support for the Republican party presidential candidate of 1928.[17]

While strictly an artistic movement, and seemingly innocuous on the political front, the Harlem Renaissance was designed to claim citizenship rights by virtue of a creative intellectual outpouring of literature, music, and painting to reveal the beauty and dynamics of the Afro-American community. For black thinkers the perception of that movement extended far beyond the promise held out by Charlotte Osgood Mason, the eccentric white spinster in mid-town Manhattan, who sponsored Langston Hughes and Zora Neale Hurston to portray blacks in their atavistic, "primitive African" sense. Afro-American intellectuals such as the NAACP's Walter White and James Weldon Johnson, both novelists of the Harlem Renaissance and University of Chicago graduate student and later head of Fisk University, Charles Johnson, viewed the artistic movement in terms of exposing the debilitating effects of racism and second-class citizenship. The fact that individuals in the NAACP and those with views compatible with this organization were involved in a cultural movement which featured such talented writers as Countee Cullen, Claude McKay, and Wallace Thurmond reflected the consciousness that literature, music, and painting could serve political purposes and vice versa. Alain Locke, for example, anticipated great social gains accompanying a "second wave" of black artistic contributions. There would be a "releasing of our talented group from the arid fields of controversy and debate to the productive fields of creative expression. The especially cultural recognition they win should in turn prove the key to that revaluation of the Negro which must precede or accompany any considerable further betterment of race relationships."[18]

In one sense or another, the UNIA, NAACP, and Harlem Renaissance leaders were inextricably linked together (though they too were capable of internecine squabbling) in their thrust for racial uplift. They were indicative, more significantly, of the growing consciousness and political awareness of the need for reform of vital importance to the larger Afro-American community. If nothing else, such groups made it apparent that there was a struggle going on in the black community for leadership of Afro-Americans, and that no one organization or individual, as had been the case during the era of Booker T. Washington, could deliver the black vote. Any political party depending on the support of the black electorate needed to consider the importance of this change both in terms of the political consciousness of blacks and the balkanization of power within the Afro-American community---something the Republican party refused to do, in any constructive and creative manner, in the 1920s. The Republican party's failure to consider the significance of this change or to explore wider political ties with the Afro-American community caused an erosion of black support after 1924. Coolidge had initiated the process of good will and appeared prepared to follow through on it, but ultimately lapsed into dependence for political advice and policy on the small residual group of black leaders formerly associated with Booker T. Washington. With this, the likelihood of the President's seeking any major racial reform policies receded into the background.[19]

Why the President turned to the Tuskegee-oriented men can best be explained by the political capital to be derived from such ties. Booker T. Washington's disciples were foremost team players in the game of politics, and had limited objectives---*viz.*, claiming more patronage jobs and assistance for institutions or communities with which they were affiliated. Politically, they could be expected to accept party decisions and mandates in the realm of race relations without any obstreperous public show of discontent. Satisfying the narrow personal objectives or professional interests of Tuskegee men was generally incentive enough for them to do the bidding of their political or philanthropic benefactors. In this sense, Tuskegee men were preeminently trustworthy.[20]

By virtue of his position at Tuskegee as successor to Booker T. Washington, Robert Russa Moton stood out initially as Coolidge's preferred adviser on Afro-American affairs, and a key person for maintaining black allegiance to the Republican party. Moton, however, had not sorted out in his own mind the nature of the role to be assumed at Tuskegee: whether to till the post in the political leadership manner of Booker T. Washington or narrow his role to that of college president interested in national affairs only to the extent that they affected Tuskegee Institute. His reluctance to involve himself more fully in politics on the national level between 1923 and 1928 prevented him from exploiting his connection with Coolidge in the fashion Booker T. Washington had done with earlier American presidents. Moton's trips to the White House during Coolidge's presidency resulted in a few suggestions for political appointments for Tuskegee loyalists, but stopped short of the systematic lobbying for patronage jobs for his followers and other machinations to exercise any significant influence within the Republican party at the national level.[21]

Within the political arena, Moton nonetheless adhered to the Tuskegee imperative of serving and appeasing powerful whites in return for favors. In 1923, while the wider black community was recoiling at the Coolidge appointment of C. Bascom Slemp as White House secretary because of his southern racial bias against Afro-Americans, Moton refused to take such a position and instead applauded Coolidge for the selection and described Slemp as a very talented person. If Moton seemed out of step with the larger Afro-American community on the Slemp appointment, his expression of confidence in Coolidge's decision was the basis of a political quid pro quo that could gain for the Tuskegee principal influence in Alabama where it was of particular importance to him. Coolidge indeed sustained the much needed commitment to Moton to allow for his prominent role in the staffing and other administrative decisions of the Veterans Hospital in Tuskegee. In April, 1926, the Tuskegee principal's secretary, Albon L. Holsey, thanked the President for this kind of support and also noted "that the trouble at the Veterans Hospital had abated since the White House became involved." Moton, however, did not go much beyond this kind of localized endeavor to exploit his relationship to the Coolidge administration.[22]

Another black political adviser upon whom the President depended was William H. Lewis, who had attended Amherst College at the same time as Coolidge. A party machine operative from the days of Booker T. Washington, Lewis early contact with Coolidge and his educational training as an Amherst man combined to ease him into the seat as an adviser to the President. Lewis managed to bask within the inner circles of the Coolidge administration for less than a year and during that period achieved the questionable honor of shaping the President's thinking on the necessity of "playing politics" with the black community. This political approach, springing from Lewis' suggestion, was directed initially at the remarkable black leader W.E.B. Du Bois, the first Afro-American to receive the Ph. D. degree in history from Harvard University and the then ranking savant and polemicist for racial justice in America.[23]

Involved extensively in Afro-American uplift endeavors and
the early twentieth century Pan-African congresses, and seeking a
more global black approach to the problems of racial bigotry in the
Americas and white colonialism in Africa and the Caribbean, Du
Bois, as editor of the NAACP's magazine, *The Crisis*, drafted scores
of penetrating essays and eloquent editorials denouncing white
prejudice and hostility leveled at blacks. Du Bois's scathing words
proved embarrassing on more than one occasion to whites and blacks
alike who vacillated on issues of racial reform. Thus in his capacity
as the *Crisis* editor, he already had been faced with several efforts in
the past to either silence or compromise him. Lewis, owing to his
political connection to the Coolidge administration, tried in vain to
coopt Du Bois in the 1920s to ensure more favorable *Crisis* editorials
on the President and the Republican party.[24]

In 1923, during the early stages of the Coolidge administration,
Lewis, in an effort to manipulate Du Bois, craftily suggested
to the President that the time was appropriate "to play a little
politics." Lewis recommended the appointment of the *Crisis* editor
as the President's special representative with the rank of envoy
extraordinary and minister plenipotentiary to the inauguration in
January, 1924 of Charles Burgess Dunbar King, President-elect of
the West African Republic of Liberia.[25] The appointment, Lewis
explained confidently to Coolidge's secretary, Slemp, "will ensure
the support of the 'Crisis' the most widely read publication among
the colored people or stullify it if it should come out against us."
Some quick scurrying by the State Department enabled Du Bois
to travel to Liberia as a representative of the United States, but the
political ruse failed to convert him into a Coolidge backer. Du Bois,
who generally remained above nostalgic party loyalties, voted for
Robert M. La Follette, the third party progressive candidate for the
presidency in 1924.[26]

But Du Bois was only one target of Lewis' endeavors to
generate more Afro-American political support for the Coolidge
administration throughout 1923 and 1924; Lewis was also
particularly keen on recommending the political appointments of
Tuskegee men of the Washington era. Demonstrating his loyalty to
Coolidge and the Republican party, Lewis anticipated receiving the
administration's high-ranking and coveted post of official political
organizer within the black community during the presidential
election of 1924. Frustrated by the loss of this position to another
prominent black in Boston, William Mathews, Lewis defected
from Republican ranks in 1924. In returning to the party almost
immediately following the election of 1924, which Coolidge won,
Lewis affected another curious *volte face*, but he was unable to regain
his former status as a major black adviser. Lewis had helped, though,
to set in motion and sanction the President's policy of "playing
a little politics" within the black community, a policy based on
the offering of limited patronage jobs and other favors instead of
substantial policy changes or reform in the interest of improving
the status of Afro-Americans.[27]

With Lewis on the fringe of the Coolidge administration after
1924, Emmett Jay Scott became the most influential Afro-American
political adviser to the President. Working characteristically in
behind-the-scenes endeavors to influence political events, Scott
guided Tuskegee political loyalists who sought recognition within
the Coolidge administration. Throughout his long involvement in
politics from the 1890s to the 1920s, Scott learned not to expect
any major or sweeping reforms for blacks. He did believe, however,
that Afro-American communities could expect piecemeal reforms in
instances where they organized themselves or when white politicians
or philanthropists were encouraged to assist them in self-help
projects. Scott began his career in Houston, Texas in the 1890s as

editor and part owner of a black newspaper, *The Texas Freeman*. He served subsequently as private secretary to Texas Afro-American political boss Norris Wright Cuney from 1894 to 1897 and then Alabama educator Booker T. Washington until 1915. During his association with Washington, Scott was recognized for his superior ability by prominent white politicians and philanthropists such as Theodore Roosevelt, Andrew Carnegie, and Julius Rosenwald. He was of such overriding importance at Tuskegee that with Washington's death in 1915, many of the black leader's followers promptly turned to Scott as the defacto head of their political machine. Scott, in fact, had narrowly missed out in the race to succeed Booker T. Washington as principal of Tuskegee Institute and a major leader of Afro-Americans between 1915 and 1917. He was catapulted into national attention, though, during World War I with his appointment as Special Assistant on Negro Affairs to Secretary of War Newton D. Baker.[28]

With the war's end in 1919, Scott received an appointment as secretary treasurer and business manager of Howard University, placing him in the nation's capital and political nerve center where he envisioned a role for himself as a powerful black political boss. But after backing the World War I army officer, Leonard Wood, for the Republican party presidential nomination in 1920, Scott suffered politically with the victory of Harding in the convention and the subsequent election. Having supported the wrong candidate, Scott and his political allies were overlooked by Harding in the handing out of patronage jobs generally occupied by blacks. On several occasions between 1921 and 1923, Scott implored Harding to appoint more Tuskegee loyalists to patronage jobs, but the black political leader's requests generally remained buried at the bottom of the list. With Coolidge's coming to office in 1923, Scott anticipated that his followers would receive patronage jobs more readily at the hands of a president expected to be more liberal toward blacks in general and the Tuskegee-oriented political faction in particular. Coolidge's first year in office justified Scott's political optimism as he and other Tuskegee loyalists drew more attention from the new President and Republican party.[29]

Scott's role became more pronounced in the Republican party, particularly in his capacity as a member of the Advisory Committee of the Republican National Executive Council. In accordance with his rising influence in the new administration, Scott scheduled a meeting for the President and White House secretary Slemp with black editors on 29 May 1924, prior to the party's national convention; there he helped to extract a pledge from the Afro-American editors to back Coolidge for the nomination and bid for the executive post in 1924. Scott's popularity and influence with the new administration were manifested on another occasion in June of 1924 prior to the national convention when Coolidge accepted an invitation to address an audience gathered at Howard University for the commencement exercise. On the platform from which the President spoke were Emmett Jay Scott and one of his ranking allies, James A. Cobb, a law professor at the institution: two black politicians determined to capitalize on their connections to the Republican party to obtain patronage jobs and financial backing for Howard University. On that occasion both men must have been heartened by Coolidge's speech in which he observed that: "Racial hostility, ancient tradition, an social prejudice are not to be eliminated immediately or easily, but they will be lessened as the colored people by their own efforts and under their own leaders shall prove worthy of the fullest measure of opportunity.[30]

As a black leader, Scott had adhered to the premise in this statement since the days of his involvement in racial uplift activities in Houston, Texas in the 1890s. His philosophy of leadership entailed a concept he labeled "constructionalism"—i.e. blacks devising policies and programs for uplift rather than merely always reaction to capricious racism whether in particular instances or more institutionalized forms. Motivated by this view of leadership in the 1920s, Scott had prevailed upon Republican party legislators in the nation's capital to obtain larger appropriations for Howard University and the subsequent recognition of the federal government's responsibility to fund the black institution yearly in a manner similar to financial aid provided for West Point and the Naval Academy. Scott's ties to white Republican politicians and philanthropists had indeed allowed him to exercise influence beyond his administrative job and responsibilities as secretary-treasurer and business manager of the black university: he became one of the leaders of the Howard clique which engineered the election of the college's first full time black president, Mordecai Johnson, in 1926. Scott's activities after 1923 centered on utilization of his political influence for educational progress at Howard, and acquisition of more patronage jobs for his political allies and followers.[31]

Scott ingratiated himself with the Coolidge administration by advising and guiding the President on ways to improve his executive image and appeal to blacks. In activities long associated with the traditional means of Tuskegee men for courting favor with white politicians, Scott influenced black newspapermen to write favorably of Coolidge and alerted the President to the importance of such endeavors. Scott, for example, wrote the President on March 5, 1927, explaining that he had mailed letters to many black newspapers and the Columbia Press Bureau pointing out Coolidge's actions in regards to the "reduction of sentence of former members of the 24th U.S. Infantry" involved in the Brownsville episode.[32]

to become even more influential with the

d it much easier to gain access to the

ation of Coolidge's secretary, C.

ary, 1925 and his replacement with Edward

Amherst alumnus who did his college preparatory

ard University and thus felt some allegiance to the

ucational institution. With Coolidge in the White House,

ott did enjoy more favor with the new president as well as the

Republican party.[33]

Tuskegee men, many of whom were Scott's closest associates, were once again given significant patronage jobs: Charles Anderson of New York as Collector of Internal Revenue, at a salary of $6,000 annually; Walter L. Cohen of Louisiana as Controller of Customs, at a salary of $5,000; and Arthur Froe of Washington D.C., as Recorder of Deeds, at a salary of $4,000. Owing in part to another of Scott's recommendations, Hallie Q. Brown, former lady principal of Tuskegee and a member of the Afro-American Club Women's movement, became Director of the Colored Women's Division of the Republican National Committee. The major political appointment Scott succeeded in obtaining for a friend, however, was that of a judgeship to the municipal court of the District of Columbia in 1927 for James A. Cobb to replace the prominent black Washingtonian Robert H. Terrell who died that year.[34]

Scott clearly was the ranking, if behind-the-scenes, black adviser to the President. Coolidge's political connection to Scott manifested itself even on a social level when in 1927 the President extended courtesies to the Howard University secretary by mailing flowers to his daughter upon her marriage to Hubert Delaney, who later ran unsuccessfully for a congressional seat in New York. (Delaney was later appointed as a judge in New York City.) Tragically, it was the death of this very same daughter later in 1927 that led to almost a year of mourning for Scott and his family and only marginal political involvement for him during that twelve-month period.[35]

Only on one or two occasions while Scott served as the major political adviser to Coolidge did he urge the President to seek some solution to the problems of lynchings and segregation. And when the President did respond to the problems of bigotry and discrimination after 1924, whether at the behest of Scott or others, his statements often had a matter-of-fact ring to them. Worse, as was the case in 1926 when he criticized the Ku Klux Klan (but not in 1925 when this white supremacist group held a major march and rally in Washington D.C.), his response sometimes appeared to be a perfunctory political exercise to merit credibility. The President did respond in other instances by pointing out the ills of lynchings once again in his speech before Congress in 1925 and, in another case, when he admonished a federal official, Winfield Scott, Commissioner of Pensions in the Interior Department, for allowing the separation of black and white employees in federal offices under his jurisdiction. But these cases represented individual reactions that held no promise of any major executive branch shift in policy or long-term directives in the interest of Afro-Americans. What the President failed to do to correct racial injustices perhaps was a more telling story. Coolidge, for example, decided ultimately to forego any endorsement of the Layton Bill and anti-lynching measure in Congress because he feared such support would jeopardize the passage there of legislation for the Mellon tax reduction act of 1924. The extent of Coolidge's retreat from his commitment to reform measures for Afro-Americans was apparent in his response to a black delegation to the White House in 1927 when he expressed apprehension that any support on his part to enforce the provisions of the Fourteenth Amendment might lead to a disruptive Senate filibustering maneuver hampering endeavors to get other legislation through the Congress.[36]

In many ways, Coolidge, as President, proved to be too much the pro-business conservative Republican trying to avoid political or social problems that might limit his ability to deal fundamentally with economic development. His administration became more conservative and preoccupied with economic expansion and development from 1923 to 1928, and accordingly less concerned with social maladies of bigotry and discrimination. In retrospect, perhaps no amount of organizational and institutional thrust of Afro-Americans could have altered this political process, but it was easier for Coolidge to lapse into his conservative posture on racial matters owing to his relationship with Afro-American politicians who were basically content with the bestowing of financial aid to institutions they represented or the acquiring of patronage jobs for themselves and their allies.[37]

The discrepancy between Coolidge's statements for racial reform and his policy of neglect of the overall interest of the Afro-American community at large fostered an acute sense among blacks that they had been betrayed. The NAACP gave clear evidence of its disappointment by passing a resolution in 1926 that Afro-American "political salvation and...social survival lie in our absolute independence of party allegiance in politics and casting our vote for our friends and against our enemies." The resolution marked a turning point in the relationship between blacks and Republicans, and revealed that traditional party strategies and ways of winning the Afro-American vote had run their course. The party of Lincoln could no longer anticipate the kind of black support it had enjoyed in previous years. This instance of black political independence and the search for an alternative had been hastened by Coolidge's policy of "playing politics" which underscored to blacks the neglect of their basic concerns by Republicans who had come to take the Afro-American vote for granted.[38]

Within the context of black political disappointment with the Republican presidential administration by the mid-1920s, Coolidge's decision not to run for the executive office in 1928 appears even more intriguing. The President's statement of "I do not chose to run," while strong, still left open the possibility of a draft movement and seems to have been a political trial balloon. Any understanding of Coolidge's personality, particularly his sensitivity and need for reassurance that he was doing a fine job in the executive office, reveals why he placed his candidacy before the American public in such a problematic way. By late 1927, prior to the nomination contest, he seemingly needed affirmation and acknowledgment from the American people that he had done a credible job. Had they come forth quickly and decisively in favor of Coolidge, it is more than probable that he would have felt obliged to honor their wish. Yet, this did not happen, and Coolidge, in the absence of a draft campaign, was left to abide by his words that he "did not chose to run. " There is, however, strong indication, owing to Coolidge's activity regarding the black community at least, that he was taking steps in the electoral interest of the Republican party or his own candidacy, given the open possibility of a draft movement in 1928. Curiously enough, it manifested itself in a political decision affecting the Black Nationalist, Marcus M. Garvey, who had been convicted of mail fraud in 1924 and sentenced to the Atlanta Federal Penitentiary where he was scheduled to remain until 1928.[39]

Garvey's followers mounted a strong effort to get him released from the Atlanta Federal Penitentiary, including the mailing of numerous petitions to Calvin Coolidge. In the midst of this endeavor, the Jamaican's wife, Amy Jacques Garvey, was approached by Robert L. Vann, editor of the highly regarded black newspaper, the *Pittsburgh Courier*, and attorney James A. Cobb, both of whom suggested rather confidently that for a fee of $5,000, they could obtain a presidential pardon for Garvey. It is probable that this was a scheme which originated with the trio of Emmett Jay Scott, Cobb, and Vann, and that all three men were depending on their relationship with Coolidge to obtain the pardon for Garvey. It can only be speculated whether they believed and suggested to Coolidge that he or the Republican party could profit politically and count on more black votes by issuing this pardon to a black leader who many Afro-Americans believed to have been victimized for his role in organizing perhaps the most significant black mass movement of the twentieth century. Given the timing of the offer to Amy Jacques Garvey, however, it is more than likely that these issues were uppermost in the thinking of Vann and Cobb. Only the large legal sum requested by Cobb and Vann led Garvey's wife to refuse their assistance to get her husband released. She eventually hired two young white attorneys for considerably less to obtain Garvey's release from jail in late 1927, some six months before his sentence was to have officially ended. The President's pardon for Garvey came, it should be noted, during the preparation for the elections of 1928.[40]

It seems correct to observe that the release of Garvey was more than just a disinterested gesture on the part of a president. It appears to have been politically motivated, a last-minute atonement to blacks and bid for their votes. Here once again was a quadrennial presidential election where the interim four years had produced hardly any constructive legislation or overall Republican party interest to warrant political support. More specifically, the decision may have been necessary owing to the long list of Afro-

Americans standing ready to renounce the Republican party in 1928. Editors of major black newspapers such a the *Chicago Defender*, *Baltimore Afro-American*, and the *Boston Guardian* all turned their backs on the Republican party, and voiced support for the Democratic presidential candidate of 1928, Al Smith. Marcus Garvey, who previously had endorsed both Harding and Coolidge, echoed the sentiment of black editors that blacks should vote Democratic in the forthcoming presidential election. And even Walter White of the NAACP suggested rather strongly that the fate of the organization hinged on the rejection of the Republican party in 1928 by the masses of black Americans. In the South also, the alliance between blacks and Republicans showed signs of weakening as indicated by Robert R. Church's open, "best-of-two-evils" political letter of 1928 in which he proclaimed that "the Republican party offers us little. The Democratic Party offers us Nothing." All of these individuals were powerful representative leaders in the Afro-American community. Their disappointment in Republican party leaders in 1928 and, in some cases, their support for Democratic candidates evinced the intensity of their political alienation from the party of Lincoln. Why presidents locked in the White House behind advisers were capable of alienating various factions and political allies, whether they be black or white, was something which concerned Coolidge and a problem to which he provided astute answers in his autobiography when he wrote in 1929: It is difficult for men in high office to avoid the malady of self delusion. They are always surrounded by worshippers. They are constantly, and for the most part sincerely, assured of their greatness....They live in an artificial atmosphere of adulation and exaltation which sooner or later impairs their judgment. They are in grave danger of becoming careless and arrogant....It is necessary for the head of the nation to differ with many people who are honest in their opinions. As his term progresses, the number who are disappointed accumulates.

Finally, here is so large a body who have lost confidence in him that he meets a rising opposition which makes his efforts less effective.[41]

Coolidge's judgment was impaired in a similar manner with blacks because he made the mistake of surrounding himself with "old guard" politicians who were a carryover from the Booker T. Washington era. And, as president, he too came to take the Afro-American vote for granted in a decade when blacks were demonstrating a capacity for new thinking and seeking other political alternatives compatible with reformist activities of the UNIA, the NAACP, and the Harlem Renaissance movement. Considering all of this, it is still an overstatement to argue, as one historian does, that the Coolidge administration was largely responsible for the shift of blacks to the Democratic party in the 1930s. Although Coolidge's policies may not have precipitated a mass exodus of blacks from the Republicans, he was largely responsible for the Afro-American political mood of despair of 1928, manifested in the feeling that little could be done to make the Republican party more sensitive to their votes and to the need for reform in their communities. The shift of Afro-American from the Republican to the Democratic part in 1936 reflected cumulative black political disappointment with the "party of Lincoln" occurring over the preceding seven decades as much as it did the search for immediate relief from the Depression of 1929 and the resulting economic and political dislocation. Coolidge, however, might have salvaged some of the Afro-American faith in the Republican party in the 1920s by a more open and continuous response to the wider spectrum of thought within the black community as he had done for a few months in 1923 and 1924. Afro-Americans were certainly not ready to take the leap of faith into the Democratic party by the latter half of the 1920s, but neither were they willing to suffer continuously with a Republican party unappreciative of their votes and impervious to their requests.[42]

(Endnotes)

1   For a cogent discussions of this question, see John Blum, *The Republican Roosevelt* (Cambridge: Harvard University Press, 1954) ; Seth Scheiner, "Theodore Roosevelt and the Negro, 1901-1908," *Journal of Negro History*, 47 (November, 1962): 169; Louis R. Harlan, *Booker T. Washington, The Wizard of Tuskegee*, 1901-1915 (New York: Oxford University Press, 1983), 3-32; Donald McCoy, *Calvin Coolidge: The Quiet President* (New York: MacMillan Company, 1967), 217,241.

2   Edward C. Lathem, *Your Son, Calvin Coolidge* (Montepelier: Vermont Historical Society, 1968), 34-40; McCoy, *Calvin Coolidge*, 1-30, 217, 241; Claude M. Feuss, *Calvin Coolidge: The Man From Vermont* (Boston: Little, Brown, and Company, 1940), 1-70.

3   "Memorandum on Important States," August 9, 1924, reel 63, Calvin Coolidge Papers, Microfilm Edition, Forbes Library, Northampton, Massachusetts; Sam Marvello, "The Migration of Blacks to the North, 1911-1918" *Journal of Black Studies*, 15 (March, 1985), 292; Daniel M. Johnson and Rex R. Campbell, *Black Migration in America: A Social Demographic History* (Durham: Duke University Press, 1981), 86-79.

4   Lathem, *Your Son, Calvin Coolidge*, 34-40; McCoy, *Calvin Coolidge*, 1-30; Feuss, Calvin Coolidge: *The Man From Vermont, 1-70.*

5   Emmett Jay Scott to William H. Lewis, 27 April 1920, cont. 18; Lewis to Scott, 30 April 1920, cont. 28; Scott to Channing Cox, 25 January 1923, cont. 24; Republican Party Campaign Broadside, c. 1920, cont. 28, Emmett Jay Scott Papers, Soper Library, Morgan State University, Baltimore Maryland.

6   Robert R. Moton to Calvin Coolidge, 17 December 1924, reel 64; Calvin Coolidge Statement, 3 October 1924, reel 64, Coolidge Papers, Microfilm Edition; Coolidge to Moton, 9 August 1923, cont. 86, Robert Russa Moton Papers, Hollis B. Frissell Library, Tuskegee Institute, Tuskegee, Alabama; Pete Daniel, " Black Power in the 1920s: The Case of Tuskegee Veterans Hospital," *Journal of Southern History*, 36 (August, 1970) 368-88; Harlan, *Booker T. Washington: The Wizard of Tuskegee*, 5-31.

7   Daniel, "Black Power in the 1920s," 368-88; Harlan, *Booker T. Washington: The Wizard of Tuskegee*, 5-31.

8   In the personal papers of Coolidge and his standard biographies by McCoy and Feuss, there is no evidence to suggest that his contact with blacks during his early days and vice presidency went beyond interaction with the Tuskegee-oriented men. For information on this topic see the microfilm edition of the Coolidge papers as well as the collection of personal correspondence located in Forbes Library in Northampton, Massachusetts.

9   John Blair, "A Time for Parting: The Negro During the Coolidge Years," *American Studies Series*, Volume 3 (London, England), 178-79; Stephen Fox, *The Guardian of Boston: William Monroe Trotter* (New York: Atheneum, 1971), 248-49; Sherman, The Republican Party and Black America, 200-23

10   C. Bascom Slemp to Moton, 22 September 1923, cont. 86; Moton to Coolidge, 15 October 1923, cont. 86, Moton Papers; "suggested Statement for the President," 4 October 1923, reel 63, microfilm edition to Coolidge papers.

11   N.D. Brascher to Coolidge, 6 November 1923, reel 63, Coolidge Papers; *Washington Eagle*, 6 October 1923.

12   Calvin Coolidge, *Annual Message of the President of the United States to Joint Session of Congress*, November, 1923 (Washington: Government Printing Press), 1-14.

13   Maceo Crenshaw Dailey, Jr., "Emmett Jay Scott: The Career of a Secondary Black Leader," Ph.D. dissertation, Howard University, 1983, 438-77; Giles B. Jackson to C. Bascom Slemp, 25 October 1923, reel 63, Coolidge Papers.

14   Blair, "A Time for Parting," 178-79; Sherman, *The Republican Party and Black America*, 200-23; Fox, *The Guardian of Boston*, 248-49.

15   James W. Johnson, *Along This Way* (New York: Viking Press, 1933), 374; Blair, "A Time for Parting," 177-99.

16   David L. Lewis, *When Harlem Was in Vogue* (New York: Vintage Books, 1979); See Tony Martin, *Race First: The Ideological and Organizational Struggle of Marcus Garvey and the Universal Negro Improvement Association* (Westport: Greenwood Press, 1976) for important discussions of the Garvey movement and the Harlem Renaissance. See also Sherman, *The Republican Party and Black America*, for an examination of the general extent to which the party of Lincoln overlooked black organizations.

17   Martin, *Race First*, 3-66; Emonei Carter to Coolidge, 8 December 1924, reel 63, Coolidge Papers; Dailey, "Emmett Jay Scott," 299-301.

18   Alain Locke, "The New Negro," in Locke, ed., *The New Negro* (New York: Albert and Charles Boni, 1925), 15.

19   For full discussions of this question see Lewis, *When Harlem Was in Vogue*; and Sherman, *The Republican Party and Black America*, 177-99; also, Blair, "A Time for Parting."

20   Harlan, Booker T. Washington: *The Wizard of Tuskegee*, 1901-1915, contains the most recent discussion of the interaction of Washington and his followers with Republican party officials.

21   Moton to Slemp, 20 January 1925, cont. 86; Coolidge to Moton, 9 August 1923, cont. 86, Moton Papers; Moton to Coolidge, 17 December 1924, reel 64, Coolidge Papers.

22   Albon Holsey to E.T. Clark, 21 April 1926. Ree; 64, Coolidge Papers; C.B. Slemp to Moton, 22 September 1923, cont. 86; Moton to Slemp, 13 December 1923, cont. 86, Moton Papers.

23   E.J. Scott to E.T. Clark, 21 January 1924, reel 139; W.H. Lewis to C.B. Slemp, 30 October 1923, reel 139, Coolidge Papers.

24   Lewis to Coolidge, 4 October 1923, reel 139; Scott to E.T. Clark, 21 January 1924, reel 139; Lewis to Slemp, 30 October 1923, reel 139; President C.D.B. King to W.E.B. Du Bois, Coolidge Papers.

25   Liberia was established by the American government in 1822 as a refuge for repatriated former slaves from the United States.

26   Lewis to Slemp, 30 October 1923, reel 139; President C.D.B. King to W.E.B. Du Bois, 7 September 1923, reel 139; Charles Hughes to Coolidge, 26 December 1923, reel 139, Coolidge Papers.

27   See "Memorandum from Perry Howard on W.H. Lewis," 1 October 1924, reel 63, Coolidge Papers.

28   Dailey, "Emmett Jay Scott," 34-127.

29   *Ibid.*, *Chicago Defender*, 14 June 1924. Dailey, "Emmett Jay Scott, "236-63, 438-77.

30   Dailey, "Emmett Jay Scott, "I-371, *passim., Chicago Defender*, 14 June 1924.

31   Dailey, "Emmett Jay Scott, "318-71.

32   Scott to Coolidge, 5 March 1927, reel 64, Coolidge Papers; McCoy, *Calvin Coolidge*, 285.

33   Feuss, *Calvin Coolidge*, 286; Scott to E.T. Clark, 21 May 1926, reel 50, Coolidge Papers; Scott to Coolidge, 6 October 1925, reel 64, Coolidge Papers.

34   "Memorandum: Appointment of Colored Men, 1926, " reel 64, Coolidge Papers; Scott to James B. Reynold, 16 October 1924, reel 63, Coolidge Papers; *Chicago Defender*, 7 June 1924.

35   Dailey, "Emmett Jay Scott," 269-70.

36   *Ibid.*, 468; Blair, "A Time for Parting," 182-84, 181; William Monroe Trotter to Coolidge, 1 August 1927, reel 64; Everett Sanders to Winfield Scott, c. September 1927, reel 64, Coolidge Papers.

37   Blair, "A Time for Parting," 177-99; McCoy, *Calvin Coolidge*, passim, 141, 306-10, 329, 257.

38   Sherman, *The Republican Party and Black America*, 224; this interpretation seems warranted also in view of previous evidence and the virtual non-existence of letters to this effect in the Coolidge Papers.

39   Lillian Rogers Parks, *My Thirty Years Backstairs at the White House* (New York: Fleet Publishing Corporation, 1961), 195-200; Martin, *Race First*, 14.

40   Martin, *Race First*, 3-19; Andrew Buni, *Robert L. Vann of the Pittsburgh Courier: Politics and Black journalism* (Pittsburgh: University of Pittsburgh Press, 1974) 232; Amy Jacques Garvey to Andrew Buni, 9 August 1971, Marcus Garvey Papers, cont., Fisk University Library.

41   Martin, *Race First*, 199-200; Weiss, *Farewell to the Party of Lincoln*, 9-12; Calvin Coolidge, *The Autobiography of Calvin Coolidge* (Rutland: Academy Books, 1972), 241.

42   Blair, "A Time For Parting," 199. For treatises on this historical issue see Rayford W. Logan, *Betrayal of the Negro: From Rutherford B. Hayes to Woodrow Wilson* (New York: Collier Books, 1965); Nancy J. Weiss, *Farewell to the Party of Lincoln: Black Politics in the Age of FDR* (Princeton: Princeton University Press, 1983); Richard B. Sherman, *The Republican Party and Black America: From McKinley to Hoover*, 1896-1933 (Charlottesville: University Press of Virginia, 1973).

BOOKER T. WASHINGTON AND THE AFRO-AMERICAN REALTY COMPANY

Generally speaking, black American businessmen have mimicked their white counterparts in seeking to establish fruitful ties with political leaders. Yet these ties have often been counterproductive for both black businessmen and black leaders. The Afro-American Realty Company, which existed from 1904 to 1909, offers an excellent prism from which to view the problems resulting from the linkage of the two. Under the hegemony of Phillip A. Payton, "The Father of Colored Harlem," the members of the Afro-American Realty Company established liaisons with the "Tuskegee Machine" and its National Negro Business League.[1] Tuskegee support marked the end of the company's incubation stage, and the directors soon turned to the very serious business of implementing the concept of black economic nationalism. But the company quickly sank into a sea of woes Blacks know only too well- unwise speculation, a depression, and an inability to woo black investors. Both Harold Cruse in the *Crisis of the Negro Intellectual* and Gilbert Osofsky in *Harlem: The Making of a Ghetto* attribute the company's collapse to the economic problems mentioned above, and Osofsky places the unwise speculatory business policies squarely on the shoulders of Phillip A. Payton. While these scholars are essentially correct, they neglect the history of the company prior to the critical year of 1909, and the company's liaison with the "Tuskegee Machine."

After 1900, Washington found it increasingly necessary to pivot toward many northern urban communities to consolidate his power, obviate criticism, and solidify his position as leader of the race. In doing this, Washington employed many tactics, from the age-old method of the "carrot and the stick" to placing the Tuskegee harness over many power-wielding agencies in northern black communities.[2] This, essentially, was Washington's posture toward the Afro American Realty Company. Thus, if the company is viewed in the proper perspective — submerged in the political and economic ambience of the Tuskegee Machine in New York - then its failure can be seen as a consequence of the political and economic reverberations as Washington's power waned in New York and his disciples mutinied.

No attempt is made here to place the livery of modern colors on Booker T. Washington. This study was undertaken to examine the relationship between a black leader and an entrepreneur, and why the two seemed irreconcilable. While it has become fashionable to aim historical periscopes at Booker T. Washington and label him an "Uncle Tom," "Trojan Horse," or "Black Nationalist," little effort has been made, excluding the research of Washington's biographers, to analyze the operational aspects of Washington's prescriptions for racial uplift. Black capitalism was a Washington bulwark against American racism and segregation, but the struggle for leadership dictated placing one's priorities in order. This, to Washington, meant leadership first, all else second.

"The Place of Failure in Business" by H.T. Kealing, editor of the *A.M.E. Church Review* of Philadelphia, was the opening speech at the second day of the New York National Negro Business League Conference of 1905. Rule four of Kealing's catechism for business success was "special friends and blood kin are the worst enemies to business success.... One cousin is worse than a dozen rats, and an uncle can do as much damage as a burglar." Yet, the black capitalists, who came to apotheosize Booker T. Washington and cash in on the concomitant benefits, paid little attention to Kealing's warning. While they probably agreed upon the dangers of blood kin and nepotism, their attendance, and possibly their silence, revealed their belief in the value of having special friends, for they were there

to pay homage to their influential special friend - "The Wizard,"
Booker T. Washington. The poignant message in Kealing's speech
probably also eluded Booker T. Washington, Emmett Jay Scott,
and Phillip A. Payton because all three were preoccupied with the
thought of staging the most successful Business League meeting
to date.

To Booker T. Washington, the National Negro Business League
was a vital part of his plans for racial uplift and penetration of
northern black urban communities. Though at the zenith of his
power in 1905, Washington was still concerned about the nascent
and nagging opposition in northern black communities. Two years
earlier, in 1903, the eminent black scholar W.E.B. DuBois had
acerbically criticized Washington's program for race progress; thus,
Washington invited DuBois and other black leaders to a New York
conference in January 1904 to reconcile opposing points of view.
Out of this Andrew Carnegie funded conference emerged an ad
hoc "Committee of Twelve for the Advancement of the Interests of
the Negro Race." This committee was an amalgam of DuBois's and
Washington's ideas for race progress. However, when Washington
appeared to vacillate on the committee's plans to press vigorously for
civil and political rights of Blacks, DuBois withdrew and sounded
the call for the Niagara Meeting of 1905. The Niagara Meeting was
a formidable challenge to Washington as a race leader; many of
the delegates came from northern and southern anti-Washington
enclaves.[3]

Somewhat disturbed by this challenge to his leadership,
Washington, in one sense, was picking up the gauntlet at the
National Negro Business League meeting of 1905 by displaying
the largest body of black businessmen heretofore assembled,
who were casting their buckets down where they were and rejecting,

what seemed to them, DuBois's abstract and jejune ideology of racial uplift.

Emmett Jay Scott's enthusiasm for a successful Business League meeting equaled Washington's. While clearly understanding the importance of having a spirited Business League meeting, Scott would have generated enthusiasm without this added incentive, for he regarded the Business League as one of the major pillars in Washington's program for racial uplift. Since coming to Tuskegee in 1897 from his post as editor of a black weekly newspaper in Houston, Texas, he had become indispensable to Washington. In addition to being Washington's secretary, Scott was a one-man cabinet.[4] He performed myriad tasks, from the collecting of data on the black community to offering advice and assurance. In 1900, when Washington announced his plan for a Negro Business League, both Scott and T. Thomas Fortune, editor of the *New York Age,* encouraged him to convene the first meeting.[5] Scott was particularly excited about the idea. The years at Tuskegee already had given him elbow-rubbing exposure to white millionaires who supported Washington, and he was beginning to exhibit the sort of "Herbert Pockets" mien that permeated his later life. At the first League meeting, Scott was elected secretary, responsible for coordinating and supervising annual meetings. Keenly aware of Washington's determination to maintain his position as spokesman for the race and to curtail any opposition to Tuskegee policies, Scott was ready to stage a production at the League meeting which would display and amplify the support Washington received from the black community.

Phillip A. Payton myopically expected more immediate and concrete rewards from the League meeting in 1905. Along with Fred Moore, a personal friend and staunch supporter of Washington, Payton shared the responsibilities for planning the conference.

Payton was determined to capitalize on this event; he knew that a well-organized meeting would impress Washington, and he welcomed such an opportunity. Payton was an ambitious and aggressive opportunist, fond of characterizing himself in the words of Robert Ingersoll, the nineteenth century agnostic and iconoclast, as being among the men introducing "irrigation into h ell and (who) were getting all there was to get out of the disadvantages their situation imposes."[6] By 1905, he was the most successful black realtor in New York City. He knew that the proper business and political ties could make him a real estate magnate in New York, and he had spent his earlier years fruitfully cultivating such ties.

Coming from Westfield, Massachusetts in 1899, Payton entered New York equipped to grapple with urban life. He had attended Livingston College and mastered the barbering trade.[7] Barbering was the second occupation he pursued in New York after losing his first job as a vendor. His third job as a porter in a real estate office gave him a glimpse of the money-making opportunities in that field, and in 1900, he and a partner opened a real estate office on West 32nd Street. However, Payton's partner withdrew from the company when its annual gross receipts totaled only $125.[8]

Continuing alone, Payton had better luck. In 1901, a dispute between two white realtors prompted one to turn his apartment complex on 134th Street over to Payton to be filled with Blacks.[9] With the drive of a neophyte and an uncanny business aptitude, Payton acquired customers and more property by such innovative ideas as placing real estate advertisements on outdoor billboards, subways, and trains.[10] As business improved, he sought to ally himself with other black businessmen and expand his business.

In 1903, he attended the Business League meeting in Nashville,

Tennessee, as a member of the nine-man business delegation from New York and delivered a speech on the "'Possibilities of the Negro in the Real Estate Field.'"[11] He argued that real estate was a door to safe and profitable investments as well as property ownership. At the same meeting, he and Wilford H. Smith, a black attorney in New York, laid before Scott their plans to expand the Afro-American Realty Company into a partnership and they encouraged Scott to get in on the "ground floor."[12] Though Scott was equivocal in his initial response, he quickly changed his mind when Payton and J. C. Thomas, a black mortician who also dabbled in real estate, combined their resources in May of 1904 to block a white syndicate's effort to evict Blacks from apartment complexes on 134th Street. Booker T. Washington praised Payton for his business adroitness and race loyalty in blocking the eviction attempt.[13] Emmett Jay Scott followed several days later with a letter referring to Payton's maneuver as a "Napoleonic feat," and subsequently requested to get into the company on the "ground floor."[14]

Under Payton's business engineering, the "ground floor" of the Afro-American Realty Company in 1904 was a partnership of 11 Blacks, the most eminent being Wilford Smith, J. C. Thomas, and James E. Garner, owner of a black janitorial firm in New York. In June 1904, the company was incorporated and authorized to issue $500,000 shares of stock at $10 each, and each of the 10 original partners received 500 shares for his interests in the partnership.[15] It was an auspicious beginning for the company, with some of the Tuskegee Machine's most prominent and successful black businessmen in New York working in a concerted effort to find desirable housing for Blacks. Payton planned to brighten the company's future by getting the direct support and cooperation of Washington and Scott.

By fall of 1904, Scott was in on the "ground floor" by purchasing $500 worth of stock (his wife purchased $100 worth of stock); and he was expected to peddle stock subscriptions to Washington and other stalwarts of the Tuskegee Machine. But Scott's inability to sell stock to Washington troubled Payton, and he wrote a personal letter to Washington explicitly stating the aims of the company and encouraging him to purchase stock.[16] Washington politely refused, but stated that he approved of the aims of the company and might consider purchasing stock at a later date. Though Washington made no personal investment in the company, he and Scott used the company to undermine a critic.

In December 1904, Scott wrote Wilford Smith instructing him to withdraw the advertisement of the Afro-American Realty Company from the *Voice of the Negro* because its editor, J. Max Barber, an inveterate critic of Washington, published a DuBois article accusing Washington of using $5 000 to silence vitriolic criticisms in five black newspapers.[17] Smith was further instructed not to show Scott's letter to Payton and to destroy it without issuing a reply. Smith withdrew the advertisement, but assured Washington and Scott that "Payton would have endorsed his actions."[18] The company was thus sucked into the vortex of Tuskegee politics. Whether Washington's Machiavellian stance toward the company would have developed anyway or whether it had been fostered by Payton's attempt to lure Scott away from Tuskegee with a lavish salary offer of $3,000 in the Afro-American Realty Company is unknown, but the company was now viewed by Washington as a potential Tuskegee vehicle.[19]

Having used the company to undermine one adversary, Washington now seemed ready to give it more support. By the summer of 1905, his followers were strategically positioned in the company. Charles Anderson, Washington's Count Chauvin in

New York, was elected vice president of the company; Fred Moore occupied the post of secretary treasurer; Wilford Smith was the attorney for the company; and Emmett Jay Scott was on the board of directors. All of these men were indebted to Washington and could be counted on as loyal supporters. Anderson held his prestigious position as collector of the internal revenue in New York largely because of Washington's influence. Both Moore and Smith were on the Tuskegee payroll, Moore as paid organizer of the Business League and Smith as attorney in civil rights cases which Washington surreptitiously funded. The only maverick among Washington's lackeys was Payton. For Payton wanted the economic influence of the Tuskegee Machine, not its political woes. Thus, he followed Tuskegee decisions to the extent that they would produce pecuniary rewards.

Earlier, Payton had displayed his maverick tendencies by supporting a New York Democrat for Congress in 1904.[20] Washington and Scott, hoping that a taste of Tuskegee hospitality would heighten Payton's reverence for Tuskegee policy, invited him to the 1905 commencement week at Tuskegee. But after being ceremoniously wined and dined by Washington and Scott, Payton remarked that his only regret was that he would have to "Jim Crow" it home. Payton was alluding to two things: the endemic nature of segregation in the South and that Washington, because of his friendships with white railroad magnates, often traveled in a separate compartment in railroad cars with the full amenities of first class fare. While Scott admonished Payton for the intemperate comment, the incident probably reaffirmed Washington's view that Payton was not completely in the fold.[21]

Tuskegee men in New York initially did not seem to share Washington's reservations about Payton. Their letters to Tuskegee during the summer of 1905 exhibited respect, fraternity, and innocuous jesting towards Payton. Fred Moore wrote Scott, "I understand *Phil* Payton *is* down at Tuskegee, and I want to give you a hint to watch him for fear that he may insist on taking you out in his automobile. Beware of him, give him all the chittlerlings."[22] Smith, turning to a nuptial theme, wrote Scott that "he was over to Payton's house, the boy had retired and had not seen him. Saw the madam … surprised that she has grown in corpulency."[23] By the fall, this fraternal relationship had ended because of a power struggle for control of the company, resignations and threatened resignations of key figures, and disagreement on business policies necessary to give the company a better financial image.

After serving as vice-president for two months, Charles Anderson resigned because he was unable to devote full time to the company, and he later secured political appointments for Fred Moore and Wilford Smith. Anderson wrote Washington that Moore's job would require him to resign from the realty company. However both Moore and Smith stayed in the company and by October 1905 they were involved in a power struggle with Payton for control of the company. Both sides sought allies at Tuskegee. Payton, hoping to replace Moore, again offered a post in the company to Scott, but Scott refused. When Moore uncovered this ruse, he wrote Washington that Scott's second refusal was a wise decision and that Payton "was down in the mouth" because of the decision. Moore also informed Washington that the company had to follow a "conservative policy."[24]

By "conservative policy," Moore meant that the company had to improve its financial image and sell more stock. While Payton agreed with Moore and Smith on these goals, he apparently wanted to achieve them by reducing the shares of stock the original company members received for their investments and also the capitalized stock from $500,000 to $150,000. The directors of the company seemed to agree that the price the corporation paid in stock to the company's partners ($50,000) was inflated and that it should be adjusted to $6,400. While this maneuver was designed to give the company a better financial image and to make the stock more attractive to the public, it simultaneously minimized the voting power of the original directors by reducing the shares of each from 500 to 64. Excluding the stock belonging to the original directors, there were only 860 shares of outstanding stock; thus, one could easily secure control of the company by purchasing a controlling share of stock or influencing the other stockholders.[25] Theoretically, both factions were in a position to secure control of the company, but Payton seemed to emerge as the dominant force in the company.[26]

The fact that Payton now seemed to be in control of the company led Smith and Moore to consider resigning. Probably more disturbing to both men was a suspicion that it was Scott's support that enabled Payton to influence others in the company. Moore and Smith discussed their proposed resignations with Booker T. Washington, and they urged Scott to tender his resignation. Scott refused to do this, though Moore and Smith proceeded with their plans to resign and continued to encourage Scott and others in the company to do the same.[27] At this point, Washington stepped in to mediate this conflict and to appease both Smith and Moore by keeping Scott at Tuskegee and thus preventing him from influencing the affairs of the company.[28]

Though the crisis had been resolved, the problem had not. The struggle for control of the company escalated briefly in 1906 while Moore and Smith were still in the company. Payton complained to Scott early in 1906 that things were going poorly in the company, and that he wanted to discuss the matter with him.[29] Scott, however, was in a delicate situation, trying to balance himself between dual loyalties for his mentor Washington and his friend Payton. Both Scott and Payton knew that Washington suspected that their friendship could undermine the Tuskegee Machine, and that Washington had decided to keep Scott away from New York. Although Washington had temporarily severed the contact between Payton and Scott, he had also hampered his ability to monitor the operation of the company for he had to rely extensively on Fred Moore for information, and Moore never seemed to be abreast of company affairs. Thus, Smith, one of Washington's key followers in the company, resigned without Washington's prior knowledge or approval.[30]

Wilford Smith's resignation in April of 1906 paved the way for Payton's control of the company. Payton consolidated his position by extending the olive branch to James A. Garner, securing Scott's reelection to the board of directors, and by purchasing the stock of J. C. Thomas (securing for himself the controlling shares of stock). Now firmly in the saddle, Payton proceeded to implement the policies he thought would facilitate the growth of the company. In July, he purchased an apartment at 525 West 151 Street and demanded that the white tenants vacate by August 1 in order to make room for black families. The white press in New York quickly responded to this ploy by accusing Payton of unveiling a nefarious and clandestine Negro scheme to invade white communities. Payton's eviction of the whites was an effort to increase the company's profits and provide more apartments for Blacks, similar to his earlier effort to block the eviction of black tenants from 134th Street in 1904.[31] This time, however, he had circumvented two of Washington's cardinal strategies - secret offensive maneuvers and counter defensive moves. Washington could not condone this. Four days later, he wrote Payton that this type of sensationalism would harm the race and that "the other race after all is the most powerful one, and it is pretty hard to say what direction they are likely to turn if they are forced to."[32] Scott also questioned this move, but to the more sympathetic Scott, Payton explained that now was the time to make his fight.[33]

The Tuskegee Machine in New York had other problem which made Washington a bit more sensitive about Payton s move, for it was beginning to reveal tensions that had remained submerged for the last few years. The mistrust, muckraking, and chaos among its members now began to surface. Washington's disciples were criticizing one another and, in the process, revealing the intricate matrix of centralization Washington had woven in New York. Charles Anderson voiced his long-held suspicions about Fred Moore and at one point described him to Washington as a "summer coon, neither fit for fur or (sic) meat."[34] T. Thomas Fortune, the brilliant but erratic polemicist for the Tuskegee Machine, publicly stated that Washington owned half of the *New York Age,* a disclosure that Washington immediately denied.[35] In the midst of these peccadilloes in New York, Scott requested a $500 loan on his stock; this may have been due to real financial need, but was more likely an effort to extricate Tuskegee from a potentially embarrassing political situation.[36]

The internal feuding which burdened the Tuskegee Machine in New York found a larger stage within the Afro-American Realty Company, and created a temporary rift between Payton and Scott. In January of 1907, Payton was arrested and charged with issuing a fraudulent prospectus from the company. The plaintiffs, Frank Armand and Charles Crowder, two former stockholders in the company, hired Wilford Smith (the former attorney for the company) as their lawyer.[37] Although Payton was personally exonerated because it was a corporate enterprise, he felt that the publicity weakened the confidence of the black community in the company. The *New York Age* (a Tuskegee instrument) candidly and comprehensively covered the story despite the fact that Payton was then on a four-man task force to incorporate the *Age* and that he was the largest subscriber to advertising space in the paper. Payton felt that the *Age's* coverage of the story of his arrest and the court case was tendentious; his suspicion of the Tuskegee men increased when he learned from Fortune (also a member of the task force) that Scott had approved that Wilford Smith, the prosecuting attorney in the fraud case, should handle the legal aspects of incorporating the *Age*.[38]

In a fiery letter to Scott, Payton accused him of double dealing. Scott, however, was quickly able to placate Payton by denying Fortune's statement and later offering Payton advice on the impending lawsuit against him.[39] According to Payton, the worst aspect of the court case was that it forced him to reveal the weak financial status of the company thereby undermining the solid and cohesive image of the company he had managed to create in the New York real estate world. The court case also reflected more of the cumbersome problems that the company inherited under the aegis of the Tuskegee Machine in New York. For the prosecuting attorney Smith turned out to be one of Tuskegee's summer soldiers in New York and no longer willing to follow blindly Washington's orders. He was looking for a chance to even the score with Payton, and was instrumental in encouraging the plaintiffs, Crowder and Armand, to press charges against Payton.[40]

By the summer of 1907, Payton spearheaded another attempt to restore a better image of the company. The progress report, issued by the company in 1906, had indicated a discrepancy between the company's financial image and its actual balance sheet; also, the company was unable to declare any dividends for its stockholders. By the end of 1906, the company housed 146 families in 13 apartment houses valued at $470,000. The total property owned and leased was valued at $1,100,000, and when all the property was rented, Payton expected total rents of $144,500. The net surplus of the company was totaled at $7,942.01, but Payton needed a better yield to declare profits and dividends and restore confidence in the company. Ignoring partisan allegiance and adhering to sound business principles, he prepared to tap all segments of the black community. He advertised in the anti-Washington paper (*The Boston Guardian*, edited by Washington's nemesis, Monroe Trotter), sought a direct written endorsement from Booker T. Washington, and encouraged Scott to write an article for his news weekly real estate bulletin which analyzed the progress of the company.[41] Payton, unfortunately, was involved in a sisyphean struggle; the company's growth had been seriously retarded by the internal problems, making it extremely vulnerable to monetary policies. Thus, the company was unable to weather the tight monetary policy during the recession years of 1907-08 in New York.[42] In the same year, three other black real estate companies in New York collapsed- the Worker's Realty Company, the Metropolitan Realty, and the Afro-American Investment Corporation. Also, white realty companies, such as the Hudson Realty Company, were accused of sabotaging black realty companies by persuading white lending firms to withdraw mortgages from black companies. L. B. Byron, writing for the Writers' Project Program in 1932, cited this as the major reason for the collapse of the Afro-American Realty Company[43] --- a contention supported by James Weldon Johnson in *Black Manhattan* and Alain Locke in the *New Negro*, both qualifying it by adding that the failure of sundry black realty companies discouraged black investments in the Afro-American Realty Company.[44] All of this occurred at a time when influential friends might possibly have helped to offset the effects of the recession. And, in light of the fact that the company had been plagued by internal dissension and "sensationalism" which discouraged investments, Payton's actions during 1907 appear more incomprehensible as he struggled to buy more apartments despite the fact that he was unable to fill those he already owned. He made it increasingly difficult for the company to meet its mortgages and made the financial crisis more acute.

In another sense, Payton's actions were understandable. He realized the company's precarious financial status, and he responded like a gambler who had lost most of his money on small bets and now, in poverty, was banking on the long shot to go home a winner. However, he should have heeded gamblers' advice that success sharpens the judgment, failure blunts it.

Payton's actions in this period seemed to be those of a panic-stricken man. By November, desperately needing a sum between $10,000 and $20,000, he planned to visit Andrew Carnegie and Oswald Garrison Villard to request funds to keep the company solvent.[45] Moore warned Payton that Carnegie and Villard were philanthropists who would frown upon aiding a business concern, and who would be particularly insensitive to the plight of the Afro-American Realty Company, since it did not charge Blacks nominal rents.[46] Unsuccessful in his attempts to see Carnegie, Payton asked Washington to secure him an audience with Carnegie. Washington adroitly adopted Moore's position, telling Payton that this was a business rather than a philanthropic matter. Washington's distinction between business and philanthropy was, at best, tenuous. He did believe in using philanthropists in business matters as demonstrated by his solicitation of Julius Rosenwald in

1909, another white philanthropist, to invest $30,000 in a black business venture which failed within a few years.[47] As the collapse of the company appeared imminent, Moore again suggested to Scott that they should resign. Scott refused to do so, and told Moore that he would stand by Payton in his time of trouble, but might resign later.[48]

As the financial picture of the company became more bleak, Payton continued to beseech Washington for aid. In late November, still seeking an audience with Carnegie, he went to Boston to meet with Washington and to renew his plea for a letter of introduction to Carnegie. But Washington demurred on the request.[49] That night, Payton and Washington returned to New York aboard the same train, and during the night, Washington sent for Payton. But Payton had retired for the night and thus was not disturbed. Payton later sensed that he had missed an excellent opportunity to lay his cards on the table, for he wrote to Scott that he was sorry he had missed a chance to have a heart-to-heart talk with Washington. Payton, nonetheless, continued his efforts to enlist Washington in his cause, and again importuned Washington for a letter of introduction to Carnegie. Washington's reply to the letter led Payton to assume that the meeting would be arranged. Thus, he composed a short history of the company to give to Carnegie. In the report, Payton highlighted the fact that the company controlled 34 apartment houses, with 23 valued at $1, I 09,711 owned by the company, and that the company housed 3,500 Blacks. Payton added that lending institutions refused to provide mortgage money, and he concluded his report with a request for a loan of $850,000 to be repaid with 5 percent interest.[50]

The composition of the short history of the company was in vain. Washington did not arrange the meeting with Carnegie. In desperation, Payton asked Washington to underwrite the debts of the company, but Washington refused.[51]

Washington's reluctance was due primarily to the fact that he saw no benefits to be derived from continued Tuskegee association with the Afro-American Realty Company. While in a position to get Payton an audience with Carnegie, it is doubtful that he had resources at his disposal to underwrite the company's debts. The fact that he did neither reflected his determination to end all ties with the company. Washington's decision may also have been prompted by the fact that Payton had attempted to entice his dependable secretary away from Tuskegee, had wrested the control of the company from Tuskegee men in New York, and had enveloped the Afro-American Realty Company in an aura of "sensationalism."[52] Thus, Washington only gave the company tacit support during its hour of need, knowing full well that its demise was imminent. He did not lend a helping hand because Tuskegee aid could only be counted on when it furthered Tuskegee aims. The Afro-American Realty Company at one time afforded Washington such an opportunity; however, by 1907, he saw no political or economic dividends to be derived from continued affiliation with the company. Indeed, it was an obvious sore thumb of Tuskegee involvement in New York.

The Afro-American Realty Company collapsed in 1908. Payton reached a nadir in his own financial situation the same year. At one point, he was in danger of losing his own house. By April, however, business picked up. Exhibiting his former business acumen and advertising skills, he published a weekly bulletin providing Blacks with articles on real estate, Negro history, and a helpful list of desirable places to live in New York. He requested Scott, in his capacity as Booker T.'s secretary, to write an article for the bulletin.

It appeared that Payton was on the road to financial recovery. Fred

Moore informed Scott that Payton was doing good business. In May, Scott wrote Payton that he was delighted to learn that his friend had "gotten his old stride again."[53] Scott's amiable tone later changed when he discovered that two former stockholders were contemplating bringing another suit against the directors of the company. Earlier, Scott had cautioned Moore and Payton to issue a public statement on the company's failure. Now his letters to them became more strident in tone, reminding them that his name had been used in support of the company, and that he and his wife had invested $600 and only received one dividend. Scott's anxiety sprang from the fact that he had been on the board of directors of the company and was, therefore, subject to any court proceedings. He beseeched Payton and Moore, as honorable men, to explain the company's failure and avoid any legal complications.[54]

Scott's anxiety heightened when he received a letter on August 1, 1908, from James E. Wetmore, a black New York lawyer and friend of Washington. Wetmore stated that he had been employed by two stockholders to investigate the Afro-American Realty Company, and that he would not mind seeing two of the company's officials (Payton and Moore) go to jail.[55]. Scott, anxious to remain out of any impending court case, replied to Wetmore that "the Afro-American Realty Company never meant anything personally so far as profiting by it is concerned."[56] The same day, he drafted a letter to Moore spelling out the tip from Wetmore and the pressure he was receiving at Tuskegee because of his affiliation with the company.[57] Moore showed the letter to Payton, and he answered Scott with a lengthy letter explaining that there was "no skeleton in the Company's closet. My connection with it has cost me my health and modest fortune." Payton reiterated his belief that the company would have been a credit to the Negro race as well as a great help, but' 'it is the old story of the saddest of all words of tongue and pen."[58]

In November, Payton consulted a law firm for advice on the Realty Company, and was advised that while there was no reason to dissolve the company, he should prepare a statement to the stockholders explaining the collapse of the company. Payton's procrastination in issuing such a statement prompted Scott to write another letter. Being pressured by Washington, Scott explained to Payton and Moore that "it is of a rather serious imprint that I should have lent my name to the Afro-American Realty Company, and while receiving no benefit from it in any way but to rest under suspicion and misunderstanding."[59]

While the formal structure of the company vanished in 1908, Payton continued in the real estate business. He still manifested business temerity on several occasions, but now he was free from the malignant mixture of business and politics which resulted from his alliance with Tuskegee men. He maintained his lasting friendship with Scott and stayed on friendly terms with Washington.

Ironically, one month before his death, Payton closed the most lucrative deal of his career, acquiring six modern apartment buildings on West 141 Street valued at 1.5 million dollars. This property was taken over by another realty company, which included several of Payton's former business colleagues (including Emmett Jay Scott) and rented under the name of the Afro-American Realty Company. Payton lived a short but exciting life, and the accolade of the' 'Father of Colored Harlem" was well deserved. Even when death came, he faced it with his characteristic panache. The New York Age reported his death and funeral September 5, 1917: "He" (Payton) loved Dunbar and his favored piece which was constantly on his lips was 'When all is Done.' On Wednesday evening, just before he passed away, he tried to sing 'Nearer My God to Thee' but was too weak. The sister asked him if she could sing it for him and she did the best she could under the circumstances. He looked her in her face and said, 'Darling, you will never be a Melba'[60]and then passed out across the bar where he met his pilot face to face."

(Endnotes)

1   Finding adequate housing facilities was a problem that had plagued black New Yorkers all during the nineteenth century and the beginning of the twentieth century. Throughout this period, Blacks had been on a forced unidimensional trek from lower to upper Manhattan, They were forced out of the Five-Point District (presently the site of City Hall in New York) by the Irish, and later ushered out of "Little Africa" (Greenwich Village today) by the Italians . At the beginning of the twentieth century, Blacks were uprooted from the Tenderloin and Juan Hill areas, from 37th to 58th Street, because of renovation and commercialization. Payton secured apartments in Harlem in 1903 and enabled Blacks to move into this area. For this, he was dubbed "The Father of Colored Harlem." See Gilbert Osofsky, *Harlem: The Making of a Ghetto* (New York: Harper & Row, 1963) and Hollis Lynch, *The Black Urban Condition* (New York: Thomas Y. Crowell Company, 1973).

2   August Meier, *Negro Thought in America* (Ann Arbor: University of Michigan Press, 1968), pp. 100-189, *passim*

3   Meier, pp. 177- 179.

4   My own research into the Booker T. Washington papers and the Emmett Jay Scott papers has convinced me that Scott had either a photographic memory or 100 percent recall. l am not going to shy away from the observation that Scott was more to Washington than merely a secretary, and that he often made decisions involving the Tuskegee Machine when Washington was away on trips. Professor Meier stated (discussion with me on March 24, 1975) that he saw a reference in the DuBois papers in which DuBois stated that he believed Scott was the head of the Tuskegee Machine. Of course, this topic needs further research; I hope to shed more light on it when I complete my research on the life of Emmett Jay Scott.

5   Samuel R. Spencer, *Booker T. Washington and the Negro's Place in America* (Boston: Little, Brown, 1955), p. 123.

6   *Springfield Republican*, May 29, 1905.

7   Payton's father was somewhat of an ambitious capitalist in Westfield; he was a barber and peddled tea and other products. The mother was a beautician. Of the four children, Phillip was the only one who failed to graduate from college. Two sons graduated from Yale and a daughter from Westfield State. The father insisted that the three boys learn the barbering trade. See Booker T. Washington, *The Negro in Business* (Boston, Chicago: Hertel, Jenkins, and Company, 1907), p. 200.

8   Osofsky, p. 94.

9   *Ibid.*, p. 202.

10   An article in the *New York Age*, July 12, 1917, credited Payton with being the first to use advertising in such a manner.

11 Negro Business League Meeting, *Proceedings*, 1903.

12 Emmett Jay Scott to Phillip A. Payton, August 9, 1904 (cont. 24); Scott to Wilford Smith, August II, 1904 (cont. 871), Booker T. Washington Papers, Library of Congress.

13 Booker T. Washington to Payton, May 3, 1904 (cont. 870).

14 Scott to Payton, May 10, 1904 (cont. 24); Scott to Payton, May 13, 1904 (cont. 24); Scott to Smith, August II, 1904 (cont. 871).

15 Osofsky, p. 96.

16 Payton to Washington, October 13, 1904 (cont. 293); Scott to Payton, October 18, 1904 (cont. 293).

17 Hugh C. Bailey, *Liberalism in the New World* (Florida: University of Miami Press, I969), p. 94.

18 Scott to Smith, December 22, 1904 (cont. 24); Scott to Smith January 20, 1905 (cont. 24); Smith to Scott, December26, 1904 (cont. 24); Scott to Smith, January 25, 1905 (cont.25).

19 Reading the letters of Booker T. Washington, one often has difficulty ascertaining when Washington is speaking through his amanuensis Scott or when Scott is speaking. The staff members of the Library of Congress initially considered titling the present Booker T. Washington Collection as the Booker T. Washington and Emmett Jay Scott Papers because of the large volume of Scott letters. Professor Louis Harlan stated (telephone conversation with me March 3, I 976) that Emmett Jay Scott was an exceptionally bright and ambitious young man, and that he harbored ideas of one day becoming a successful black businessman and leader. Within the Tuskegee framework, Washington gave Scott a great deal of latitude in joining and supporting black enterprises such as the Afro-American Realty Company. Scott, in an effort to get Washington's support for the company, probably had to demonstrate that there were advantages in identifying with Payton and the company. The use of the company to undermine J. Max Barber was an effort in this direction. To what extent Scott influenced Washington's decisions in reference to the company is unknown. I hope to unravel the relationship between Scott and Washington in my dissertation. No doubt, Professor Harlan will shed a great deal of light on this topic. Scott to Washington, October 27, 1904 (cont. 293); Washington to Scott, ca. October or November, 1904 (cont. 24); Speeches at testimonial dinner for Emmett Jay Scott, April 30, I 952, Special Collection, Davis Room, Morgan State College.

20 Moore to Washington, November 10, 1904 (cont. 29).

21 Scott to Payton, ca. May or June, I905 (cont. 30); Payton to Scott, February 19, 1904 (cont. 24).

22 Moore to Scott, May 22, I 905 (cont. 847).

23 Smith to Scott, July 10, 1905 (cont. 5).

24 Moore to Washington, September21, 1905 (cont. 29); Moore to Washington, July 26, I905 (cont. 29); Anderson to Washington, October 10, 1905 (cont. 27); Anderson to Washington, November 12, 1905 (cont. 27).

25 Stock Adjustment Report, ca. I 905, (cont. 47).

26 Scott was angry at Moore for his failure to mail the minutes of the meetings of the board of directors, and he threatened to resign if Moore continued to be derelict in these business matters. Scott also

offered his stock to Wilford Smith at half price ($250). These measures, of course, can be interpreted in several ways: they could have been threats to make Moore more business-like in dispatching his duties; Scott could have been showing his displeasure with Moore and Smith; he, knowing that Smith and Moore might resign because of their loss of influence in the company, could have been offering his stock to them to increase their power in the company. Scott generally sided with Payton on questions involving the managing and selling of company stock, so offering his stock to Smith may have been a show of faith and an effort to reconcile the two factions. What is important here is that these issues reflected the internal chaos in the company and the inability of its members to work as a cohesive business unit. An enterprise plagued with such personnel and administrative problems would find it difficult to implement judicious and profitmaking business policies. Scott to Moore, December 12, I 905 (cont. 29); Scott to Smith, December, I 905 (cont. 5); Moore to Scott, December 27, 1905 (cont. 29); Payton to Scott, December 4, I 905 (cont. 30); Scott to Moore, December 7, 1905 (cont. 29).

27 Scott to Payton, December 4, 1905 (cont. 30); Moore to Scott, December 27, 1905 (cont. 29).

28 Scott to Payton, April24, 1906 (cont. 335); Payton to Scott, April30, 1906 (cont. 335); Scott to Payton, February 16, 1906 (cont. 335); Scott to Payton, May 6, 1906 (cont. 335).

29 Payton to Scott, January 9, 1906 (cont. 331).

30 Scott to Moore, January, 1905 (cont. 335); Scott to Smith, May 8, 1906 (cont. 335); Scott to Payton , May 3, 1906 (cont. 335).

31 Article New *York Times.* July21, 1906, p. 30.

32 Washington to Payton, July 25. 1906 (cont. 331).

33 While the evidence is inconclusive, it is possible that Washington. maybe in an effort to monitor or influence policies more closely, invested in the company after 1906. The letters between Moore and Washington reveal the shifting and transferring of funds in New York; there were two notes for $250 and $600. At this same time Washington, in a rather angry letter to Moore, demanded the minutes of the meetings of the Executive Committee of the Afro-American Realty Company. See letters between Washington and Moore July 6 1906, October 27. 1906, November 3, 1906, November 2. 1906 (cont. 33); Payton to Scott, August, 1906 (cont. 4); Scott to Payton August 7, 1906 (cont. 335).

34 Anderson to Washington. April 13, 1906 (cont. 2).

35 Spencer. p. 161-166.

36 Scott to Payton. August 8, 1906 (cont. 335).

37 Atwell to Scott, February 4, 1907 (cont. 37).

38 Payton to Scott. October 31, 1906 (cont. 356).

39 Scott to Payton, February 9. 1907 (cont. 356); Scott to Fortune, February 9, 1907 (cont. 37).

40 Smith to Scott, February 16, 1907 (cont. 37); Payton to Scott, October 31, 1906 (cont. *356);* New *York Age,* January 31, 1907, February 7, 1907.

41 Short history of the company, Booker T. Washington papers, (cont. 356); Moore to Scott, December 12, 1906 (cont. 330).

42 Osofsky, p. 102.

43 L. B. Byron, WPA Project *Unpublished Papers,* Schomberg Collection, NewYork Public Library.

44 James Weldon Johnson, *Black Manhattan,* (New York: Amo Press, 1968), p . 149.

45 Osofsky, p. 59.

46   Moore to Scott November 26, 1907 (cont. 36).

47   E. Franklin Frazier, *Black Bourgeoisie*, (New York: Macmillan, 1969) p. 138.

48   Scott to Moore, November 20, 1907 (cont. 36).

49   Payton to Scott, Novernber 30, 1907 (cont. 356).

50   Washington to Payton, December 2, 1907 (cont. 356); company history, ca. 1907 (cont. 356).

51   Payton to Scott, March 30, 1908 (com. 41).

52   Certainly something else was troubling Washington about the Payton-controlled Afro-American Realty Company other than the fact that black businessmen should not expect aid from white philanthropists. Also, it must be pointed out that Washington was having difficulty controlling some of the Tuskegee men in New York. Smith no longer seemed under Washington's spell and he made some rather shady moves when Washington attempted to transfer his stock in the *New York Age*. Fred Moore was perfunctory in dispatching his duties, and Washington was growing increasingly impatient with him. These two men had been instrumental in solidifying the bonds between the Afro-American Realty Company and the Tuskegee Machine. It was Smith who first helped Washington and Scott to use the company for political ends. By 1908, Smith and Moore were eyed suspiciously by Washington and Scott. Thus, Washington's refusal to help Payton was influenced by these problems and also an effort to either extricate Scott from affiliation with the company or part of a mutual decision between Scott and Washington to end visible ties with the company. The basic point is that Payton didn't receive help from Scott or Washington at this critical juncture.

53   Moore to Scott, April 7, 1908 (cont. 41); Scott to Payton, May 12, 1908 (cont. 356).

54   Scott to Moore, July 25, 1908 (cont. 379).

55   James Wetmore to Scott, August 3, 1908 (cont. 384).

56   Scott to Wetmore, August 5, 1908 (cont. 384).

57   Scott to Moore, August 5, 1908 (cont. 379).

58   Payton to Scott, August 7, 1908 (cont. 379).

59   Scott to Payton, December 12, 1908 (cont.41) .

60   Payton was referring to the diva Nellie Melba who consumed small crackers to contain her weight. The crackers later became known as Melba crackers.

THE AFRICAN UNION COMPANY OF THE 1920S AND ITS BUSINESS ACTIVITIES IN AFRICA AND THE UNITED STATES [1]

With the formation of the African Union Company, African American entrepreneurs reached into their ancestral homelands seeking markets, profits, and opportunity at the onset of the twentieth century as some had done in less ambitious ways during the latter half of the 1800s. The economic direction of this company, the business proclivities of its founders, and the pioneering foray into foreign markets reveal much about the high level of organizational and institutional development in the African American community from 1900 to 1930 and the value of the visionary leadership in developing a credo pointing to global profit opportunities. In little more than three decades of perhaps the most fascinating eras of African American History (with the exception of the eras of Abolitionism, Civil War and Reconstruction, and the "1960s"), many of the boldest black leaders bestrode the American stage, exceptional institutions and organizations took shape and form, and the thick wall of segregation and bigotry was being chipped away at its base. Business development was quickly called into play as the struggle for uplift and reform intensified in black American communities to the degree that the era can be seen as "The Golden Age of Black Capitalism," as Professor Juliet E. K. Walker so aptly characterizes it. [2]

The African American capitalist and entrepreneurial ethos was remarkably directional and dedicational from 1900 to 1930, driven clearly by the beliefs that money and profits could be used to build a significant black community as well as challenge the anti-democratic spirit that led to lynchings, denial of opportunity, and limited public conveniences for African Americans. John Hope, Brown University alumnus and then professor at Atlanta Baptist College for men (later Morehouse College), gave voice to this view of black capitalism most passionately at the Atlanta University Conference of 1899 convened by Harvard-educated genius W.E.B. Du Bois. At the advent of a century clearly evincing "the problem of the color line, "of which Du Bois spoke, Hope sought to inspire and motivate, waxing eloquently on the theme, "We are living among the so-called Anglo-Saxons and dealing with them. They are a conquering people who turn their conquest into their pockets. . . To say the least, the policy of avoiding entrance in the world's business would be suicide to the Negro. . . As a matter of account, we ought to note that as good a showing as we have made, that showing is but as pebbles on the shore of business enterprise." If expansion and profits were important to Hope, critical also were civility and a caring brand of black capitalism.[3]

The young Hope, who phenotypically could pass for white, went on to express his beliefs in a redemptive and saving grace role for African American business individuals. He believed that African American entrepreneurs "as a race, most likely will not be of the same nature as that of the Anglo-Saxons. . . [Black Americans'] emotional and spiritual elements that presage gifts . . . [are] more ennobling and enduring than factories, railroads and banks." African American business individuals were being called decidedly to accountability by Hope and charged with humanizing, rather than wantonly harpooning the world on their way to profits and wealth. Would Hope's charge stand as African Americans sought markets, domestic and foreign? Would they pursue either the so-called white man burden in Africa (pivoting to it as former black missionaries in subscribing to the view of the continent's backwardness) or provide some more sanguine approach to make capitalist liaisons between those of African descent on both continents viable and productive? Some answers are inherent in the examination of the African Union

Company as black Americans and Africans had to consider more fundamentally the consequence of capitalism and imperialism as the twentieth century began to take off.[4]

The African Union Company came out of the worldview and movement of Booker T. Washington followers and racial politics embedded within his so-called Tuskegee Machine for rewarding friends and punishing foes. Booker T. Washington and his immediate disciples rightly came to see business development and expansion as avenues to African American uplift and development. Their concerns, evolving essentially out of the late nineteenth-century discussion on black business (especially the formation of commercial organizations for unity and group uplift endeavors) led significantly to the ambitious call, meeting, and establishment of the National Negro Business League in Boston in the summer of 1900 where over three hundred African American entrepreneur-minded individuals gathered. One can debate whether the organizational idea for the NNBL was stolen from W.E.B. Du Bois and those gathered in the Atlanta conference John Hope addressed so eloquently and inspirationally, but it is impossible to deny the importance and significance of the National Negro Business League in fostering both dialogue and developmental projects to increase the number of African American entrepreneurs and point them decisively to profit-making possibilities. During the remaining fifteen years of Washington's life and leadership in the aftermath of his establishment of the National Negro Business League, he never witnessed the apex level of attainment for the organization that he first envisioned, but the National Negro Business League did sound the appropriate call for collective uplift, kept blacks focused on business opportunities, obtained support from prominent white capitalists such as Andrew Carnegie and Julius Rosenwald, and contributed to the creation of many business projects that encouraged the recirculation of African American dollars into their communities for the continued generation of jobs, services, and goods. Chapters of the National Negro Business League indeed could be found as far afield as Africa, indicating the widespread fame of Booker T. Washington.[5]

Within the framework of cooperative black capitalism and business development, the African Union Company was established in 1909 in Cincinnati, Ohio, amidst significant population growth of the black community there, one that increased each decade from 1900 to 1930 to 5%, 7%,10% of the overall city's population and which in real numbers meant 19,639; 30,079; and 47,818 respectively. The company proved to be one of the more novel economic projects within the black community and the National Negro Business League. It was founded in a city with a dynamic African American community as business, educational, and many other social institutions were established. Black Americans there had managed to survive and thrive despite an historic draconian white assault on their community in the 1830s that led to a significant black exodus from Cincinnati. Reading clubs, health care facilities, fraternities, and sororities, along with traditional organizations and institutions, all emerged to enhance the vitality of the twentieth-century Cincinnati black community. Business expansion and development were looked to as parts of the rebuilding strategy for progress. In referring to business opportunities, Wendell P. Dabney, an early self-published black historian of the city, noted in his book *Cincinnati's Colored Citizens: Historical, Sociological and Biographical*, that black merchants there had "in order to succeed, pull down the signal of distress," Trade with me because I am colored,' and erect the flag of victory, 'Trade with me because I am best." With the Cincinnati black community giving clear signs of bustling African American commerce and business leading to the formation of the African

Union Company, and as it sought to conduct its affairs from the business district and address of the Mahogany Room at 17 West 8th Street, the firm's establishment came at the fortuitous moment of renewed ties between African Americans and Africans as Booker T. Washington's amanuensis and right-hand man, Emmett Jay Scott, concluded an important trip to Liberia, West Africa, and returned poised to explore commercial and other ventures on the mother continent. Cincinnati's African-American companies realistically prepared to engage profitably in business in Africa almost a century after similar commercial activities on the continent of noted African American abolitionist Paul Cuffee and later comparable efforts by others in the latter half of the nineteenth century.[6]

The founders of the African Union Company were two enterprising and highly motivated African American capitalists, Joseph L. Jones and Charles Chappelle, who moved to incorporate the firm in 1913, only four years after its founding. Both men appeared eminently qualified, by temperament and training, to conduct the business they had established. Born in Cincinnati, Ohio, in 1868, Jones completed Gaines High School in 1886, served as Deputy Recorder of Hamilton County and principal of Douglass Night School, and founded the Central Regalia Company, all prior to graduating from Sheldon Business College in 1909. Jones was also a member of the National Negro Business League. The African Union Company represented a new stage and grand idea in the career of the enterprising Jones, who looked beyond American borders for business opportunities. His business partner, Chappelle, is the more mysterious of the two. Though African American, Chappelle was apparently the go-between residing in Africa, and charged with making the contacts and working through the fine points of business projects and agreements, a branch manager, so to speak. His letters and advice to Booker T.

Washington's secretary, Emmett Jay Scott, revealed a person with a fine business mind, able to read the motives of people as well as the meaning of balance sheets. As twentieth century pioneer black businessmen turning to Africa, Jones and Chappelle seemingly had the partnership and credentials to warrant great success. With the African Union Company's mission centered on providing business profits for black Americans, rather than taking up the black man's burden in any missionary sense in West Africa, Jones and Chappelle sought like-minded other individuals equally apprised of the capitalist opportunities. The addition to the company's board of directors of Emmett Jay Scott, Booker T. Washington's powerful amanuensis, insured greater development and commercial competitiveness of the African Union Company.[7]

Leaving his Houston community in the 1890s, where he had risen to prominence as a newspaper owner, editor, and Republican politico, Scott was invited to join Tuskegee Institute as private secretary to Booker T. Washington. Young, brilliant, and with a fine appetite for political intrigue, Scott stood to many as "suave, " exceptional in his loyalty to Washington, and, in some quarters, "the brains of the Tuskegee Machine." Above everything else, Scott's opportunism was abundantly displayed within the realm of business, and he was determined to share in any venture that had the capacity of bringing him significant income or profits. He had been a major force in the formation of the National Negro Business League and labored more than any other individual doing the planning related to annual meetings of the organization, taking care of inviting speakers and presenters, identifying conference themes, and getting reports of the events in national newspapers. At the nerve center of Tuskegee and the closest assistant and confidante of Booker T. Washington, Scott, as publicist and co planner in programmatic endeavors, had an excellent command of local, national, and global issues related to race relations, and was called upon frequently to stand in for his boss in policy meetings with powerful, prominence, and wealthy individuals. Scott reached a pinnacle in his own Tuskegee leadership career in 1909 as he traveled to Liberia, West Africa as replacement for Booker T. Washington and at the head of a delegation to assist that country in resolution of its problems growing out of limited financial resources and political instability. Scott developed an acute awareness of African issues owing to his work on behalf of Liberia. At crucial points in his career, dating back to 1897 and a trip to Washington D. C. to meet with United States Naval Under-Secretary, Theodore Roosevelt, about European encroachment on Liberian land, Scott made the 1909 pilgrimage to the small West Africa Republic, and labored for American and international financial support for the country immediately upon his return to America, later during World War I, and again in the 1920s. He addressed the question of Liberian and African development at an extraordinary conference sponsored by Clark University on its campus in Worcester, Massachusetts, and later published several tracts on the need for aid to Africa. Of the American black leaders of that period, Scott was more advanced than most in both his thinking and knowledge of Africa. There was no missionary sentimentality on his part. The Booker T. Washington philosophy to which Scott subscribed and which he enunciated centered on helping Africa emerge as a stable political place to contest the racist arguments that blacks were incapable of political governance, and on this Tuskegee-inspired crusade, Scott layered his own personal ambitions for making a little private profit in the deal.[8]

Scott readily assisted Chappelle and Jones in obtaining West African land that included palm oil plantations and mahogany timberlands. The African Union Company, in fact, seems destined

to reap great profits with the inclusion of Scott, but World War I
disrupted its smooth and orderly business as operations came almost
to a standstill. Scott himself was distracted with duties as Special
Assistant on Negro Affairs to Secretary of the Army, Newton Baker,
the highest government appointment held by any African American
leader. The economic and political dislocation brought on by
the war therefore impacted upon the African Union Company.
In another vein, however, it helped as Scott's comprehension of
business possibilities expanded as he sought to assist a World War
I Liberian delegation to the United States (almost identical to his
role in 1908 with a Liberian diplomatic group that came to America
while he was working at Tuskegee) to obtain a sizable American loan
for internal development and growth after the Liberians, seeking
to enhance their own cause and support for the loan proposition,
declared war on Germany.

By the end of the conflict, it was apparent to Scott that Africa had
major investment opportunities. Notably and opportunistically,
therefore, he argued for African independence at a significant
New York City rally, where among other platform dignitaries and
speakers was Theodore Roosevelt. On the issue of whether African
nations were to become a protectorate of the victorious European
powers, Scott emphatically said no at a time that the other great
African American human rights crusader W.E.B. Du Bois endorsed
the Western colonial scheme and status quo for a set period of
time until African leaders gave evidence of their preparation for
self-government. While the inimitable scholar and indomitable
legendary human rights activist W.E.B. Du Bois thought in limited
ways in arguing for European held African protectorates in the short
run, Emmett Scott, heir to the Booker T. Washington leadership
mantle, argued for immediate African independence and control
of the homeland by indigenous populations. "Not only are the

African colonies not to be turned back to Germany, but to no other nation as well," proclaimed Scott at the New York City Carnegie Hall gathering on November 2, 1918 in which former President Theodore Roosevelt and other dignitaries seeking leadership capital addressed the audience on the particulars of post-World War I treaty negotiations, Scott's concern in the matter may have been a mixed blessing for Africans though, for it clearly fell short of pure altruism. Promoting independence as Scott did would make it possible for direct black American economic ties with African leaders and statesmen, without the complication of the third party of European powers. Not wanting to deal with the obstacles and representation of England and European national economic interests in Africa, Scott and the company managers thought they might fare better after World War I in resumption of normal operations to amass the immediate capital needed to purchase African commodities and transport the items to United States-based companies willing to market the products in America.[9]

With mixed motives of a reformer and profit seeker, Scott indeed had sought earlier to exploit investment opportunities in the West African Republic of Liberia, and in so doing earned the inexorable suspicion of that country's leaders, themselves guilty of disturbing mismanagement and expropriation of their national wealth. While Scott was unwilling to stoop to (or get caught at) the level of disgrace as Liberian leaders, he nonetheless did not intend to live a mere notch above the poverty line or enjoy just mere middle class African American comfort. He wanted great wealth, and Africa represented a place to plant financial seeds for large investment returns. Scott stepped to the fore quickly to lead an effort to persuade two successful white American business firms, Steinhardt and Kelly, and Frank and Pinera, to finance or purchase contracts in commercial cooperation with the African Union Company. In arguing for this arrangement, Scott outlined a plan "for the future preparation and control of Liberian coffee," readily distributing it to American export and import trades to show them the profits to be had and the benefits of a business partnership with the African Union Company. In the late 1919 and early 1920, Scott's efforts were to no avail, as American white business export and import investment concerns (owing to isolationist sentiments and hesitancy to explore opportunities in foreign countries) kept their distance. Africa to many of them seemed unstable, and few could predict how much change there would be there, given the impact of World War I and the embryonic movement for African independence.[10]

Needing investment dollars, Scott was greatly tempted therefore to honor the request from Charles W. Chappelle to bring in a major Tuskegee white patron and supporter, Sears, Roebuck, and Co. magnate Julius Rosenwald, to save the African Union Company in December of 1921 when its operating funds were depleted and the firm was bordering on collapse. Having turned to Rosenwald for such support earlier in attempts to shore up other black capitalist ventures, however, Scott ultimately decided against another significant plea and replied to Chappelle that "Mr. Rosenwald of Sears, Roebuck, and Company . . . does no foreign merchandising." Scott did turn, however, to two New York firms of Levison and Company and the Finance Trust Company in efforts to convince them of likely and future profits in providing monetary assistance to the African Union Company. In both instances, though, he received negative replies.[11]

Optimism, however, soon abounded in the company a year later with the possibility of a major commercial deal in Sekondi, Ghana, in December 1922, as Scott, Chappelle, and Jones succeeded in establishing a deal for the American foreign investment firm of

Frank and Pinera to buy one thousand tons of cocoa beans from the
African Union Company's proposed acquisition of the commodity
in West Africa and then resell of the product in the United States.
To facilitate the purchase, the firm of Frank and Pinera agreed
to buy the cocoa beans at three cents a pound and help establish
a credit of $70,000 in the Bank of Britain in Sekondi to enable
the African Union Company to pay for purchasing, loading, and
shipping of the product to America. The exploration of business
opportunities in Sekondi was an excellent choice by the managers
and owners of the African Union Company. The regional surf port
city in the furthermost western region of Ghana was beginning to
grow and develop, and to rise in prosperity in the aftermath of the
building of a railroad to transport valuable mineral, gold, cocoa,
and timber from the Ghanaian hinterlands to the shoreline for
ocean shipping to buyers globally. The economic vitality of this
region was evident in other ways, even in Europe as the number
of African countries listed on the French Bourse stock exchange
increased from 22 from 1900 to 1914 to over 107 prior to the
worldwide depression of the 1930s. The exporting of groundnuts
from West Africa was becoming the principal commodity for the
French, constituting respectively in 1920, 1925, and 1928, 63%,
60%, and 53% of the total commodities extracted from its colonies
in West Africa. There should be no doubt that the black businessmen
in the African Union Company had read correctly the opportunities
for commercial wealth and profits by seeking the transport of cocoa
beans to America, and were operating in one of the most promising
commercial regions of West Africa. The 1920s, indeed, were known
as a "boom" economic period for European and western business
entities in that part of Africa.[12]

The United States side of the equation proved to be the problem,
as Frank and Pinera had difficulty in getting an American bank to

consent to providing funds for the deal since the African Union Company had "no financial rating." The enterprising Stuart Frank, however, prevailed upon Otto Kaspar of the Kaspar State Bank to arrange credit for the deal, but when Kaspar went to his "corresponding bank in Chicago" to make provisions for the credit arrangement, the institution's president suggested that it would be prudent to "wire the Bank of British West Africa in New York to ascertain if the moral responsibility of the [African Union] company was good." Though the Bank of British West Africa's New York branch president replied with an ambivalent "report that not alone was unfavorable, but…indicated a great risk by establishing credit in favor of the African Union," Otto Kaspar and Stuart Frank decided to proceed with plans to provide the funds, Frank wrote to Joseph L. Jones, "The question now in my mind is if we do establish credit immediately, can Mr. Chappelle arrange with the Bank in Seccondee [sic] to place him in position to get these Beans ready for shipment when our inspector arrives [for] the banks will assume no responsibility, not even wanting to be a party to establishing credit through their institution, so what we really have to do is to give our representative the money to pay over as soon as he arrives in Seccondee [sic]." Complicating any role by The Bank of British West Africa to assist in the deal were certainly its set amount of currency to use in the colonial region, its low reserves for the years 1921 and 1922, and, additionally, the fact that many of its business customers were draining money from Africa by redeeming their financial notes in the central office in London.[13]

Despite the gallant efforts of the officers and managers of the African Union Company, they were unable to consummate the deal for bringing the cocoa to the United States, and the firm faced bankruptcy again in January, 1923. During this month, Scott tried to rescue the company from financial ruin by turning to Edward

C. Brown, the Philadelphia African American investment and real
estate broker. Inundated with his own financial problems, Brown
found it impossible to consider helping another African American
entrepreneurial project. Miraculously, Scott, Jones, and Chappelle
maintained the African Union Company in business until 1926 by
sheer dint of their determination and optimism, fueled no doubt
by growing business opportunities in a heated American economy
of the 1920s. This was an era where many capitalists looked upon
their task as similar to Jesus, "who took twelve men from the bottom
ranks of society to forge them into an organization to take over the
world."[14] That same crusading gospel touched Scott and his business
associates in the African Union Company, and they were counting on
investment dollars in a climate, as one of Scott's Atlanta informants
advised him, where "colored people have gone stock crazy." This
bit of hyperbole may not have been that wide of the mark when one
considers the spectacular black nationalist and economic movement
of Marcus Mosiah Garvey or substantive business endeavors in
other black communities such as Atlanta, Birmingham, Chicago,
and Durham. Few Black Americans, however, looked to Africa as
ambitiously as did the company led by Jones, Chappelle, and Scott,
and they continued efforts for investment dollars to keep the firm
afloat until some big deal could be negotiated. [15]

In 1926, the trio of Scott, Jones, and Chappelle persuaded
Robert L. Vann, the prominent black attorney of Pittsburgh and
leading owner/editor of the influential African American newspaper
the *Courier*, to take over the legal affairs of the African Union
Company and assist in placing it on sound financial grounds. The
choice of attorney was a curious, but probably correct one growing
out of economic Pan Africanism. Vann was then involved with Scott
and a cabal of combined District of Columbia and Massachusetts
black leaders to intercede with the American President Calvin

Coolidge on behalf of Marcus Garvey, specifically seeking his early released from the Atlanta Federal Penitentiary where he had been sentenced for mail fraud. Attorneys Vann and James Cobb of the District of Columbia (the latter a powerful colleague and friend of Scott at Howard University) approached Garvey's wife, Amy Jacques Garvey, proposing that for a fee of $15,000 they could obtain a pardon and early release from jail for her husband. Vann's alacrity in joining the African Union Company revealed more about the pragmatism of making a living than the higher commitment to principles pertaining to the progress of diasporic descendent Africans. His Pan African spirit of cooperation being invoked to aid Garvey was governed by the same instant money and profits possibilities as in the case of the African Union Company, all adding to the problem of whether he could function well on behalf of the African Union Company. While the company's collapse, soon after Vann came on board, must be seen primarily within the context of limited access to capital (which Professor Juliet Walker argues was one of the main impediments to growth and development of black businesses), it must be placed also within the framework of mixed motives and black American dabblers in business such as Emmett Jay Scott and Robert Vann. Not forced to earn their livelihood alone in the world of capitalism, Scott and Vann increased the perils of black businesspersons seeking alliances with educators, editors, and others not directly involved in entrepreneurial activities. Yet, given the racism and limited opportunities of the time (and the seldom safety valve of being able to fail more than once), one cannot see how such alliances could have been avoided. The scarcity of resources prompted the search for support in political and social institution arenas that had many potential pitfalls, and greater possibilities of vitiating projects in their infancy. Many of the black capitalists who did succeed in grand fashion had tunnel vision in their business determination. Such singularity, when coupled with ability and work ethos, generally augured well for black businesspersons, but this was a luxury the African Union Company did not have.

The greater lesson for African Americans and African business persons today looking toward their homeland for opportunity and wealth would be to exercise real caution vis-à-vis the political systems and similar alliances, recognizing that in an increasingly global economy, the pitfalls will be more problematic and debilitating unless great forethought is given to the wide array of issues related to the formative stages of ambitious plans and projects. But "apropos of Africa," to use the fine words of Rhodes Scholar and Howard University African American scholar Alain Locke, business beckons for individuals of African descent on both sides of the Atlantic as never before, and history lessons must serve as guides for potential greater economic development and social and political progress.[16]

(Endnotes)

1   The wonders of the conference papers listed on the internet made it possible for Mr. Samuel Nketsi-Tabiri of Ghana to query me by e-mail about his great-great grandfather's investment in the African Union Company in April, 1915 in "Gold Coast now Ghana in West Africa in a town called Dunkwa." Writes Mr. Nketsi-Tabiri on 26 December 2000: "I have been trying to investigate whether the above named company still exist. In the course of my search on the internet I came across a paper you presented on November 6...[my mother] has asked me to check if the company still exist. This company was incorporated under the laws of New York with a capital stock of &500,000." In a follow-up e-mail dated 29 December 2000, Mr. Nketsi-Tabiri explained, "It was not until the last two years that I found the certificate during one of my visits to my mother in the village....I decided to pick up the certificate to Accra, the capital city of Ghana...to make inquiry from Registrar of Companies De-partment....But I did not get any good response from them....[T]he share price was $25 and he bought 2 shared April 2, 1915. The treasurer who signed the certificate was John Birch and the President was Charles Chappelle." E-mail correspondence, Samuel Nketsi-Tabiri to Maceo Crenshaw Dailey, Jr., 26 and 29 December 2000; Maceo Crenshaw Dailey Jr., to Samuel Nketsi-Tabiri, 28 December 2000.

2   Juliet E. K. Walker, *The History of Black Business In America: Capitalism, Race, Entrepreneurship* (New York: MacMillan, 1998), 182-225. This paper is explorative, given the importance of the topic and the dis-appearance of much data to sustain a more systematic analysis. Extant data for this African business history is virtually nonexistent, and it was little better given the period of time in African American history, as letters and correspondence were limited to ranking leaders rather than the "ordinary" individuals.

3   David Levering Lewis, *W.E.B. Du Bois: Biography of a Race* (New York: Henry Holt, 1993), 220; Leroy Davis, *A Clashing of the Soul: John Hope and the Dilemma of African American Leadership and Black Higher Education in the Twentieth Century* (Athens, GA: University of Georgia Press, 1998), 118-19.

4   Ibid.

5   Maceo Crenshaw Dailey, Jr., "Emmett Jay Scott: The Career of a Secondary Black Leader" (Ph.D. diss., Howard University, 1984).

6   Louis R. Harlan and Raymond Smock, *The Papers of Booker T. Washington*, vol. 12 (Urbana: University of Illinois Press, 1989); Wendell P. Dabney, *Cincinnati's Colored Citizens: Historical, Sociological and Biographical* (Cincinnati: The Dabney Publishing Company, 1926); U.S. Department of Commerce, Bureau of the Census, *Fifteenth Census of the United States*, 1930, vol. 2 (Washington, D.C.: U.S. Government Printing Office, 1931), 67; Thirteenth Census of the United States, 1910, vol. I (Washington, D.C.: U.S. Government Printing Office, 1914), 208. The evidence suggests that Scott had some discussion with Chappelle and/or Jones for establishing the African Union Company upon his return from Liberia, but there is no conclusive information to sustain this conjecture.

7   Ibid.

8   James Waller, "Emmett Jay Scott: The Public Life of a Private Secretary" (Master's thesis, Morgan State University, 1971), 35; Dailey, "Emmett Jay Scott," 298-317.

9   Waller," Emmett Jay Scott," 35.

10   Dailey, "Emmett Jay Scott," 298-317.

11   Scott to Frank, 11 September 1919, cont.16; Steinhardt to Scott, 3 April 1920, container 21; Frank to Scott, 11 May 1920, cont. 16; Scott to J. L. Jones, 11 August 1921, container 21; Frank to Scott, 13 August 1921, cont. 26; see also "Outline of Plan for Future Preparation and Control of Liberian Coffee," ca. 1919, cont. 31; Scott to Chappelle, 1 December 1921, cont. 24; Chappelle to Scott, 1 December 1921, cont. 24; Scott to President of Levison Company, 20 December1921, cont. 24; President of Levison Company to Scott, 27 December 1921, cont. 27; all in Scott Papers, Morgan State University.

12   E.C. Brown to Scott, 11 January 1922, cont. 35; Frank to Scott, 7 July 1921, cont. 26; Scott to Frank, 13 October 1921, cont. 26; in Scott Papers; *The Columbia Encyclopedia*, 5th ed., (New York: Columbia University Press, 1994).

13   E.C. Brown to Scott, 11 January 1922, cont. 35; Frank to Scott, 7 July 1921, cont. 26; Scott to Frank, 13 October 1921, cont. 26; in Scott Papers; R.S. Sayer, *Banking in the British Commonwealth* (London: Oxford University Press, 1952), 430-44.

14   This description is taken from Bruce Barton, *The Man Nobody Knows* (New York: Grosset and Dunlap, 1925). Barton praised Jesus handsomely as a businessman: "He picked up twelve men from the bottom ranks of business and forged them into an organization that conquered the world." Quoted in William Leuchtenburg, *Perils of Prosperity* (Chicago Press, 1958).

15   Scott to Cobb, 9 November 1921, cont.24; Chappelle to Scott, 1 December 1921, cont. 24; Chappelle to Scott, 5 December 1921, cont. 24; Scott to Frank, 8 December 1921, cont. 26; in Scott Papers. See also Leuchtenburg, *Perils of Prosperity*, for a discussion of the business boom period of the 1920s. See also Waller, "Emmett Jay Scott." For the most recent cogent discussion of black business and political institution building and growth during the era of segregation, see Lynne B. Feldman, *A Sense of Place: Birmingham's Black Middle Class*, 1890-1930 (Tuscaloosa: University of Alabama Press, 1999).

16   Ibid. One should note the names of individuals such as Johnson of Johnson Publishers and Regi-
nald Lewis of Beatrice in the modern era, and C. C. Spaulding and Alonzo Herndon from the turn of
the twentieth century. See Andrew Buni, *Robert Vann of The Pittsburgh Courier* (Pittsburgh, PA: University of
Pittsburgh Press, 1974), 120-232;Adelaide Cromwell Hill and Martin Kilson, *Apropos of Africa: Sentiments
of Negro American Leaders on Africa from the 1800s to the 1950s* (London: Frank Cass, 1969), 350-58).

THE BUSINESS LIFE OF EMMETT JAY SCOTT

Emmett Jay Scott was private secretary to Booker T. Washington and later became secretary treasurer of Howard University. He was involved in numerous business activities, ranging from the establishment of the National Negro Business League to the founding of an investment clearinghouse, an insurance company, and an overseas trading firm. Scott also promoted the black township of Mound Bayou and backed African American entertainment enterprises. His business activities were largely unheralded, and the frustrations he encountered illustrate both the obstacles and the opportunities for black entrepreneurs in the first half of the twentieth century.

Emmett Jay Scott, Booker T. Washington's secretary and advocate, was a leading figure in the early-twentieth-century African American business world. His determination to promote business development in the black community drew him into an impressive range of activities, and his story illustrates the vitality of black enterprise from 1900 to 1930 and also the hardships faced by black entrepreneurs. In 1900 Scott became one of the founders of the National Negro Business League (NNBL). He helped to shape the Standard Life Insurance Company of Atlanta, and he also directed the Allied Industrial Finance Corporation. Among his other projects were running the African Union Company, an overseas trading company, and promoting the Mound Bayou black township. Scott was one of the most prominent African American leaders within the framework of the evolving "group economy," a term used by historian August Meier to describe the campaign by black Americans to buy and sell to one another in the early decades of the twentieth century.[1]

Scott's fascination with business opportunities and their role in African American economic development can be traced to his formative years in Houston, where, as a young man, he worked in the city's central business district cleaning the offices of the *Houston*

Post. Later, in the 1890s, he helped to establish the *Texas Freemen,* one of the leading black newspapers west of the Mississippi. Scott viewed business entrepreneurship as a means of uplift for black Americans, both individually and collectively. He worked throughout his life as a promoter, investor, manager, and facilitator. His grandiose ideas and projects for advancing African American capitalism made him notable in this era, and, like his mentor Washington, his faith in the ability of black capitalism to overcome racial oppression enabled him to excel to a remarkable degree.[2]

Scott was born in Houston in 1873. His father, Horace Scott, had been brought to Texas during the Civil War by the man who was reported to be both his owner and his father. Scott's mother, Emma Kyle, was born in the small Texas town of Rosharon and moved to Houston during the Reconstruction period. Horace worked as a laborer for the Houston and Texas Central Railroad. He and Emma met and married about a year before Scott was born, and they settled in Houston's Fourth Ward in an area known as "Freedman Town." They had nine children; Emmett was their first.

After his early schooling in Houston and a brief stint (from 1887 to 1889) at Wiley College in Marshall, Texas, Scott returned to his hometown to start a newspaper for the black community. After founding the *Texas Freeman* in 1893, he became secretary to the powerful African American politician Norris Wright Cuney, a position that gave him the opportunity to witness the dynamic growth that was taking place in the Houston-Galveston section of Texas. Scott married Eleanor Baker of Galveston in 1897. Their marriage resulted in five children, all of whom graduated from college.[3]

At the age of twenty-four, Scott landed the plum position of private secretary to Booker T. Washington, who was then principal of the Tuskegee Normal School and Industrial Institute in Alabama.

Scott had praised the "Atlanta Compromise" speech given by Washington in 1895, in which the Tuskegee leader acknowledged the appalling conditions for blacks in the South but urged African Americans to accept the existence of segregation and forgo, at least for the short term, pushing for civil and political rights-saying, famously, "In all things that are purely social we can be as separate as the fingers, yet one as the hand in all things essential to mutual progress." In particular, Scott admired Washington's idea that blacks demonstrate their individual and collective progress through building solid institutions and strong organizations within the African American community.[4]

Within a few years of taking the post, Scott became Washington's chief confidant. The two worked together closely. Scott oversaw the governance of Tuskegee during Washington's frequent absences, and he helped to oversee the famous "Tuskegee Machine," which was both a network of African American institutions, writers, and businessmen and a system of patronage. Scott worked on speeches for Washington, and the two coauthored the book *Tuskegee and Its People: Their Ideals and Achievements* (1905).[5]

When Washington decided to make the National Negro Business League (NNBL) the centerpiece of his program of reform and uplift for black Americans, Scott provided both intellectual and administrative support; he hoped that the league would foster commercial development.[6] Scott, and other black leaders, had promulgated the idea that business growth presented an effective strategy for uplift.[7] Scott had witnessed the formation by whites of two organizations that promoted economic community development: the Houston Commercial League (1890) and the Houston Business League (1895). In 1899, Scott and Thomas Fortune, a ranking black newspaperman and adviser to Washington, counseled Washington to take the lead in establishing a similar type of association.[8]

Washington then called for the first meeting of the NNBL in Boston in 1900. The conference, which Scott helped to plan, attracted more than 300 African American businesspeople, inaugurating a central component of Washington's educational endeavors. League meetings were soon held each year, generally alternating between northern and southern sites. Black businessmen and women came from around the nation to share success stories, describe economic opportunities, establish partnerships, discuss strategies for increasing consumption, and promote the spirit of capitalism in the African American community. In 1915, the year of Washington's death, the NNBL claimed more 40,000 members and 600 chapters.[9]

From 1900 to 1915, during the height of Washington's influence, Scott contributed energetically to the development of the NNBL. He encouraged interaction between representatives from northern and southern states, rallied support for businesswomen, and promoted what later became known as "double-duty dollar" campaigns, which urged African Americans to refuse to "spend a dollar" where they could not get a job. Scott successfully solicited contributions to the NNBL from prominent white businessmen, such as Andrew Carnegie and Julius Rosenwald of Sears, Roebuck.[10] Rosenwald met Scott on his first visit to Tuskegee in 1911. The following year he returned with an entourage of philanthropists from Chicago. Subsequently, Rosenwald corresponded principally with Scott about the school's affairs.[11]

Along with his work for the NNBL, Scott promoted Washington and Washingtonian ideas about African American progress in articles and editorials. He also published, sometimes anonymously, pieces designed to quiet Washington's critics, and acted in other ways to maintain support and loyalty among members of the Tuskegee Machine.[12] Throughout Washington's life, Scott's devotion remained steadfast, and he even turned down opportunities to serve as president of other institutions in order to continue his support of the "Wizard of Tuskegee."[13] His unfaltering loyalty made Scott the target of criticism, especially after 1900, when Washington's call for a moderate response to segregation came under attack by other black leaders, such as William Monroe Trotter and W.E.B. Du Bois. But that loyalty also kept Scott at the center of Tuskegee's activities.

In the years after Washington's death in 1915, Scott faced several hurdles, some brought about by his own actions, some resulting from the demise of Washington's broader vision. His first setback occurred when Tuskegee's board of trustees selected Robert Moton, a protégé of Washington from Hampton Institute, to become principal of Tuskegee. Some trustees felt that Scott had served too long in a secondary position to be an effective leader.[14] Moton became a competent director of the school but never achieved the national prominence that Washington had.

With Tuskegee's educational affairs under Moton's control, Scott decided to direct the political and economic spheres of Washington's Tuskegee empire. As a result, the NNBL also became the site of a power struggle between Moton and Scott.[15] Scott wrote to a colleague in 1919, "Every time I turn around there seems to be the thought on somebody's part that in one way or another I ought to be supplanted or eliminated."[16] This fear was borne out when Moton promoted his own supporters in elections for the top positions and, in 1921, succeeded in becoming president of the league.[17]

Through the years, Scott and Moton remained outwardly cordial, but they were always suspicious of each other. Moton believed that the ambitious Scott had never reconciled himself to the loss of the principalship and feared that he might undermine the new administration. Scott felt that Moton was too slow in seizing the opportunities presented by his leadership position and believed that he knew better how to advance black progress, both personal and collective, in the South.[18]

The onset of World War I gave Scott the opportunity to take a leave of absence from Tuskegee and assume the post of special adviser on Negro affairs to the secretary of war, Newton D. Baker. This was the highest wartime post awarded to an African American. As both spokesperson and ombudsman for the African American community, Scott sought to improve the condition of black military personnel and to foster patriotism among African Americans. He wrote one of the first early comprehensive books on African American involvement in the war, *Scott's Official History of The American Negro* in *The World War* (1919).[19]

But in this endeavor as well, Scott received a setback. He was criticized by the NAACP *Crisis* editor, W.E.B. Du Bois, for failing to press more strongly for civil rights and racial reform for blacks in the military. Du Bois had visited France in 1919 and was angered by the racism and segregation in the United States Army that he witnessed on that trip. In the May 1919 issue of *Crisis*, Du Bois took Scott to task for not using his position to better the conditions of black soldiers: Was Scott aware of the treatment of black soldiers in France? If not, why did he fail to find out? If he knew, what did he do about it? Du Bois followed this criticism with another barb in the July edition of the paper: "If he [Scott] could not act publicly, could he not have passed the word quietly to his friends?" Scott responded, defending his actions in the *New York Age* on July 21, 1919.[20]

Later in 1919, Scott settled into a position as secretary treasurer and business manager of Howard University, where he remained for many years, working in various capacities.[21] During the 1920s and 1930s, he maintained a rigorous schedule of fundraising and other administrative work at Howard. In addition to these appointments, Scott concentrated on promoting African American capitalism and also was personally engaged in a series of business ventures. Following Washington's death, Scott had written to a friend that the African American struggle for uplift since the Civil War had been characterized by two successive stages: "oratory" and "education." In Scott's view, the next important phase would be "commercial" effectiveness.

Scott had some reasons for optimism about the coming era. Black owned business had grown rapidly in the early twentieth century. A report entitled "The Half Century of Progress of the Negro in America," published by archivist Monroe N. Work, charted African Americans' improving economic circumstances from 1866 to 1922: home ownership increased from 12,000 to 650,000; farm ownership grew from 20,000 to 1,000,000; the number of businesses surged from 2,100 to 60,000; literacy increased from 10 percent to 80 percent; and the number of churches expanded from 700 to 45,000.[22]

Scott was also encouraged that purchasing power among African Americans had increased in the early twentieth century; he saw this as an opportunity to develop a viable separate economy, with black businesses catering to black customers. The promise of this strategy was shared by many other progressive black leaders of the time.[23] August Meier described black enterprise as experiencing "a shift, underway by 1900 and completed during the 1920s, of the economic base of Negro business from primary dependence upon white customers to primary dependence upon Negro customers."[24]

Scott was engaged in areas in which black businesspeople had become active: insurance, entertainment, and financial services. His own commercial success was modest, a fact that may be attributed to his heavy personal involvement in so many different political and educational activities and to the gap between his own optimistic vision of capitalism and the economic realities that he and other black Americans faced. Among other things, his story illustrates the extreme difficulty African American businessmen encountered in raising the necessary capital to found companies.[25]

Financial Institutions

Throughout his years at Howard, Scott occupied himself with business opportunities. The Standard Life Insurance Company of Atlanta best exemplifies the inherent problems and contradictions that marked Scott's involvement in the world of black capitalism. African American insurance companies were an outgrowth of mutual aid societies, which emerged in the antebellum South to provide funds to free blacks and slaves, enabling them to tend to their sick or bury their dead with a modicum of dignity. Free blacks also maintained mutual aid societies in their communities, frequently through their churches. The line of major black insurance organizations extended from the African Union Society of Newport, Rhode Island, starting in the 1780s, to Charleston's Humane Brotherhood, founded in 1843, to the True Reformers of Virginia in the 1880s, to North Carolina Mutual in the 1890s, and finally to the Atlanta Life Insurance Company, founded shortly after the turn of the twentieth century.[26]

No black insurance company, however, started with more fanfare than the Atlanta-based Standard Life Insurance Company. Scott hoped that its founder, promotional wizard Heman E. Perry, would take the firm to unprecedented heights. Scott joined Perry in the business; by the end of the 1920s, there would be some thirty-two legal reserve insurance companies serving black Americans.[27]

Scott and Perry had been childhood friends in Houston. Scott saw himself as both gadfly and guardian to Perry. While recognizing Perry's genius for planning new companies, he believed the Atlanta businessman was not always the best person to run a firm once it was established.

Perry proposed to form the company, which eventually became Standard Life, in 1909. Scott equipped him with letters of recommendation and helped him to raise money through the sale of stock. By 1911, Perry had managed to raise $70,000 of the $100,000 necessary to begin the Standard Life Insurance Company in Georgia. Having failed to raise the legal amount required, Perry decided to return the money to investors. Unfazed, he redoubled his efforts, this time appealing to important "race men," such as the wealthy Atlanta barbershop proprietor Alonzo Herndon, who personally invested $5,000. By 1913, Perry was finally able to raise the necessary amount and open the company.[28]

The company had strong initial success. Standard Life agents wrote ordinary life-insurance policies totaling $22,881,575 by 1923. The yearly income came to $1,083,152, and Standard Life reaped cash profits of $78,910. The same year, the company declared a semiannual dividend of $6.00 on each share of stock. The board of directors decided to increase the capital stock to $250,000, thus enabling the company to meet the minimal capitalization requirement of $200,000 that it needed to do business in northern states.[29]

By 1923, Standard Life's business had extended into Alabama, Missouri, Texas, Tennessee, the District of Columbia, Arkansas, Kentucky, Mississippi, and Florida. The renovated Odd Fellows building on Atlanta's Auburn Avenue (the street housing the largest concentration of black businesses in any community) became the company's palatial headquarters. Walking into the building, as one black reporter observed, gave an African American an instant jolt of pride. Articles on Perry appeared in the *Atlanta Constitution* and in *Forbes* magazine; the latter's positive profile of a black entrepreneur was a first in the white-owned publication.[30]

Perry's brash personality became legendary. J. B. Greenwood, an Atlanta employee of Standard Life, reminisced: "Well, he did not smoke or drink. The only habit he had is he was hard to deal with." Even W.E.B. Du Bois, in his *Black Trilogy*, remarked on Perry's outgoing style, noting that he "got hold of colored men who had some savings or a business and especially of the professional Negroes and laid before them his scheme for an old line insurance company." Du Bois himself supported the Standard Life Insurance Company, purchasing an insurance policy valued at $10,000. Scott worked diligently to help Perry, and he was fairly confident that Perry's aggressive marketing would help Standard Life produce profits.[31]

Scott, who had moved to Washington, D.C., in 1919, was too far away to control or monitor Perry as the Standard Life Company entered its most promising phase. Indeed, the physical distance between the two had a negative impact on business planning and execution, since, according to their private correspondence, Perry did not always report faithfully to Scott, who was a member of the board, and Scott was unable to attend all executive meetings.[32]

In addition to serving on the company's board, Scott was also an insurance agent, receiving a 2 percent commission on all the indemnity policies he sold (buying one for his son Emmett Jr. and persuading friends around the nation to buy others). Scott bought company stock, purchased and sold insurance policies, and promoted Standard Life in letters to prominent persons and newspaper essays.[33] But he did not find his association with the company completely satisfactory, and he had to remind Perry on several occasions to send his commission and dividend checks. When Scott was unable to attend board meetings, he preferred mailing his proxy vote to his trustworthy and obedient brother-in-law, Thomas Ferguson, rather than to Perry.[34] Scott also was concerned that Perry paid too little attention to the competition. He reminded him, in August 1922, "Would it not be better for Standard Life to 'break into' Delaware before the North Carolina Mutual and the Lincoln-Douglass Life Insurance Company, a new organization, get into this field?" Scott's tone became more plaintive as he monitored the progress of competitors, such as North Carolina Mutual. Mailing North Carolina Mutual's publicity sheet to Perry, Scott strongly implored him, "For the Lord's sake do not let them get ahead of us, simply for the sake of a few dollars."[35]

While continuing to prod Perry to pay more attention to managing the company, Scott embarked on an ambitious publicity campaign of his own, submitting newspaper articles on Standard Life to major African American publications, such as the *Norfolk Journal and Guide,* and to the official newsletter of the NNBL. Scott even used a pseudonym, "E.S. Jay," in his newspaper campaign in order to protect his reputation at Howard University and to deflect any criticism that might result from engaging too heavily in business activities while at the school.[36]

Scott's campaign helped to push Standard Life to the pinnacle of its success in the mid-1920s, and he constantly urged Perry to use the company's resources to explore the possibility of developing other businesses in the black community. Perry's brand of black economic nationalism was perhaps the most ambitious of anyone's up to that time. Perry earned the nickname "Commercial Booker T. Washington," but he did so partly through adhering to Scott's advice. Scott's influence in the company was so pervasive that he once had to quell rumors that he planned to accept a post as either president or secretary treasurer.

Meanwhile, Perry was expanding in other directions. In 1917 he started an umbrella organization, known as the Service Company, which oversaw the operations of several subsidiary firms, including a realty company, a publisher, a laundry, and a construction concern. These companies, known collectively as the Service Enterprises, built homes in West Atlanta. Collectively, in the early 1920s, they employed 2,500 workers, 2 percent of Atlanta's black population.[37]

Scott aided Perry in attracting other nationally prominent black businessmen to support the Atlanta business project. In January 1923 Robert E. Jones, editor of the *Southwest Christian Advocate,* Henry A. Boyd, president of the Citizens Saving Bank and Trust of Nashville, and businessmen W.F. Boddie, H.C. Dugas, and J. M. Frierson met in Atlanta to discuss the direction of the Service Company. They rallied behind it as a profit-making venture and an excellent community-service initiative.[38]

Scott promoted the company in local newspapers. From 1922 to 1923, according to Scott, the Service Company's resources increased from three to five million dollars. He concluded: "The potential worth of this financial program speaks for itself. Its financial returns, its employment of hundreds of capable colored men and women, and its proof that the race can conduct financial concerns of this magnitude justifies the slogan of 'Service' which permeates the activities of these corporations."[39]

Perry did not limit himself to these ventures. In 1921, he had established the Citizens Trust Company Bank in Atlanta. The bank provided mortgages and loans to African American entrepreneurs.[40] Scott worked with Perry on many of his projects and also tried to establish his own large financial company in Washington, D.C. In 1921, he started the Allied Industrial Finance Corporation, a financial holding company and clearinghouse that used its capital to underwrite home mortgages, business projects, and banking establishments. Promoting the organization largely through black churches, Scott initiated a campaign to raise capital through the sale of stock.[41] A broadside announcing Scott as speaker at the Ebenezer M.E. Church in Washington on May 21, 1923, stated that the Allied Industrial Finance Corporation planned "to provide money to enable our people to buy and build homes, and to engage in business or extend and increase in present business." But although it attracted some interest, the company kept afloat only for a few years before folding in 1925.[42]

With Perry caught up in so many activities, Scott became increasingly concerned that he was not properly managing Standard Life or providing him with accurate information about the company's welfare. He went so far as to enlist people to spy on Perry. Scott befriended one of the firm's secretaries, Edyth Williams, and persuaded her to pass information to him on a regular basis. Scott also obtained information about Standard Life activities from his brother-in-law, whom he had helped to secure a cashier's job; eventually Ferguson became acting treasurer of the company.[43]

Scott was ultimately unsuccessful, however, in convincing Perry to be careful in managing his multiplying businesses. His careless oversight was particularly damaging to Standard Life. As one employee, L.D. Milton, reflected, Perry was guilty of "disobeying *three laws:* 1) the law of expansion, (2) the business cycle, (3) the law of capital structure."[44] Another employee, John A. Copeland, said that Perry "was an excellent organizer, but he was not a supervisor. He could not handle money. He ruled with iron hands. He was a dictator ... an adventurer. He would make a debt to pay a debt." Perry indeed was a great entrepreneur, but he was not up to the task of managing and directing a huge financial conglomeration once it was formed. On one occasion, he reportedly only "read the assets sheets and (threw) the statement of liabilities into the wastebasket." This recklessness proved costly, and Standard Life, in particular, faced a maelstrom of problems.[45]

One problem arose because Perry had inflated Standard Life's assets by including a large amount of foreclosed real estate, and he did not curb this practice, despite the Georgia Insurance Department's warnings to do so.[46] He also suffered a major embarrassment in December 1923, when it became known that he was seeking a deal with white-controlled Mississippi Life to take over the company. He was booed out of Standard Life's office in Memphis by his employees, who were aware of the bargain he planned to strike.

As Scott eventually discovered, Perry's empire was on the verge of collapse by the mid-1920s. The Service Company had drained the resources of Standard Life. Historian Alexa Benson Henderson points out that, despite having more than $22 million of insurance in force, more than $1 million in annual premium income, and total assets of $2 million in 1922, Perry's cash-flow problem threatened to destroy the business.[47] In 1924 Scott received an urgent telegram from Perry asking him to "come to Atlanta immediately. Conference important matter."[48]

To save Perry's empire, Scott and the board members devised the strategy of forming a syndicate to purchase Standard Life's shares in order to avoid a hostile takeover bid by the white Southeastern Trust Company. The plan never came to fruition, however. In a subsequent effort to save the company, Perry, with the encouragement of Scott and others, attended the 1924 NNBL annual meeting, hoping to find much-needed financial support, either from members or from a group of white businessmen and philanthropists. Indeed, powerful white business leaders seemed inclined to help the fledgling Standard Life, but Perry was concerned about the price they would exact for their support.[49] He vetoed the offer of a temporary loan from Julius Rosenwald, Clarence H. Kelsey, John D. Rockefeller, and Trevor Arnett to stabilize Standard Life-a loan that Scott himself had helped to arrange with the assistance of John Hope of Morehouse College. The lenders wanted a commitment that Standard Life would be more fiscally responsible and that Robert Moton would be installed as the company's head, an idea that Perry could not fathom.[50]

At this point, Perry could do nothing to forestall or prevent Standard Life's bankruptcy. It was taken over by a white-owned company, Southern Life Insurance.[51] Citizens Trust was reorganized under new management in 1924, and most of the companies that collectively made up the Service Enterprises in Atlanta, went their separate ways.[52] Scott's own Allied Industrial Finance Corporation was also dissolved in 1925.[53]

Other African American Enterprises

While Scott was active in promoting Standard Life, he also sought ways to encourage overseas trade and to promote the all-black township of Mound Bayou. Neither effort proved successful as he, again, found it difficult to obtain sufficient investment capital. His efforts in overseas trade began while he was still working for

Washington at Tuskegee. In 1913 he founded the African Union Company, a trading company that aimed to build alliances between African and African American businessmen. His partners were Joseph L. Jones, an Ohio businessmen and former deputy recorder of Hamilton County, and a partner in Africa, Charles Chappelle.

The company was dormant during the years of World War I. But by 1919 Scott and the other partners revived it by finding capital to purchase African commodities, especially palm oil and mahogany, and transport them to the United States.[54] Scott turned to two New York business firms, Levison & Company and the Finance Trust Company, for monetary support, but they both turned him down.[55] He then enlisted the support of the American trading firm, Frank & Pinera, convincing them, in 1922, to buy one thousand tons of cocoa from the African Union Company to sell in the United States. Frank & Pinera agreed to buy cocoa at three cents a pound from the company and establish a credit of $70,000 at a West African bank to allow for further purchasing and shipping of products. But the African Union Company's officers were unable to arrange for shipment of the cocoa to the United States. The loss of this big deal sealed the company's fate. As the company teetered on the edge of bankruptcy in early 1923, Scott struggled to save it. He managed to keep the African Union Company afloat for a few more years, even attracting Robert L. Vann, the Pittsburgh attorney and newspaper owner, to assume control of the company's legal affairs. By 1930, though, the African Union was defunct. Once again, the partners' inability to raise sufficient funds undermined the company, causing it to miss its one significant opportunity to capitalize on a major business deal.[56]

Scott also invested in the all-black township of Mound Bayou, Mississippi-a place that tested his faith in the viability of a separate black economy; here his returns were, again, modest. Isaiah Montgomery, a former slave of Jefferson Davis, founded Mound Bayou in 1887. African Americans there established banks and other businesses, built homes, and started schools. Booker T. Washington was a vocal supporter of the town and helped to attract business there. Its ranking businessman was Charles Banks, who used his own business, the Bank of Mound Bayou (founded in 1904), to provide important community development loans. Washington hailed Banks as "the most influential Negro businessman in the United States" and "the leading Negro banker in Mississippi." The town was aided by white philanthropists, especially Julius Rosenwald, whom Scott convinced to invest in the mill.

The town grew to have a population of 4,000 in 1907. For a shining moment, it was an exemplar of Washington's philosophy. By 1919, the state-insured town bank was once again doing business. The cottonseed- oil mill seemed on the path to success when it repaid half of a $15,000 loan from Rosenwald and cleared the mortgage debts of the firm. After a downturn during World War I, Banks was able to revitalize both the cottonseed-oil mill and the bank. On January 1, 1920, Scott received dividend checks for $321 and $231 from Banks, and he anticipated receiving similar dividends for the next decade.[57] By 1920, the company had fifty employees, and the town's future seemed bright. Mound Bayou voted a $100,000 school bond, constructed a Baptist Church for the cost of $15,000, and founded a cooperative store; a branch of the Federal Farm Loan Banks also opened in the town, and Banks looked to "King Cotton" to continue to stimulate Mound Bayou's economy.[58]

Mound Bayou's development depended on the economic vitality and prosperity of the bank and on cotton production. Between

1920 and 1922, however, cotton prices fluctuated drastically. New Orleans prices, for example, reflected a decrease from 41 cents a pound in April 1920 to 13 cents in December of that year. Prices rebounded to an average of 28 cents a pound, significantly below 41 cents. The impact on Mound Bayou was felt immediately. Charles Banks had provided $100,000 in loans to the town's cotton farmers and manufacturers. Plummeting cotton prices made it difficult for such debts to be repaid.[59] Scott tried to assist Banks by borrowing $50,000 from the War Finance Corporation, an emergency agency organized by Congress, but the corporation's directors ultimately rejected the loan application based on an official policy of not lending any bank more than twice the amount of its capital.[60]

Support from Banks helped Mound Bayou to survive, though it never really thrived. Scott used his political and economic influence to keep Banks afloat in the Mound Bayou township. Scott, perhaps, would have been wise to draw back from supporting Banks, or indeed from micromanaging the political and economic activities of the town, but his desire for profits and his admiration for the ambitious Banks propelled him forward. When Banks died in the mid-1920s, Scott essentially ceased his activities on behalf of Mound Bayou.[61]

The Entertainment Industry

Finally, Scott's broad-ranging interests in African American economic independence encompassed the entertainment industry as well. From the 1920s to the mid-1930s, Scott became involved in several black cultural endeavors. One was the Pace Phonograph Corporation, which produced records under the Black Swan Label in the 1920s. Having helped Harry H. Pace and "Father of the Blues" William C. Handy establish the record company, Scott promoted the firm. On one occasion, he tried to persuade I. S. Rosenfels, the merchandising manager of Sears, Roebuck, to sell Black Swan records in his department stores, but Rosenfels peremptorily rejected the proposition. By 1922, the Pace Phonograph Corporation's annual net profits had reached $10,857. It employed an office and shipping staff of fifteen and seven district sales managers working in various American cities. Pace once claimed that it shipped 2,500 records every working day. The company's best-known singing group was the Black Swan Troubadours, featuring the up-and coming jazz performer Ethel Waters. Other rising black musicians who recorded on the Black Swan label were Ivan H. Browning, the lead tenor of "Shuffle Along," and the sassy female artist Alberta Hunter. Scott also persuaded Pace to record the Howard University Military Band.[62]

Though Pace's company had extraordinary early success in producing and marketing records by black American jazz, blues, and gospel performers, it was displaced by white businessmen with greater capital.[63] The company folded in late 1923, as it was unable to compete with Okeh, Columbia, and Paramount.[64]

Scott was also involved in the movie industry, working as a consultant for the New York based Constellation Film Corporation and as a member of the advisory board of the Monumental Corporation. He also collaborated with Claude Barnett, founder of the Nile Queen Movie Production of Chicago Picture Corporation.[65] Throughout the 1920s and 1930s, Scott was preoccupied with making a film on the life of Booker T. Washington. Scott and Ben Tallon of Metro-Goldwyn-Mayer tried to get King Vidor (then touted for his extraordinary scenes of black lifestyles in the movie "Hallelujah") to direct the film and Paul Robeson to star. Scott mailed Robeson a copy of the biography, observing that he would "find that he and the Founder of Tuskegee Institute after all, are not very far apart"; but despite this astonishing assertion, he never succeeded in signing him.[66]

Scott's interest in movies prompted him to help struggling African American film producers. He especially admired the work of filmmaker Oscar Micheaux, who fearlessly explored a wide range of black life in contemporary America. In the early 1920s, Scott recommended Micheaux's movies to several theater owners and, on at least one occasion, initiated an advertising campaign for one of his films in Washington, D.C. Troubled by the failure of Micheaux and his aides to provide circulars and brochures for the advertising, Scott eventually halted the campaign for fear of ruining his own credibility.[67]

Scott forged a strong alliance with black film producer George Frederick Wheeler, whom he called an individual with "the greater sympathy and knowledge of the Negro question and its manifold angles." With Scott's encouragement, Wheeler moved to California to get his film career off the ground following the failure of his movie *Birth of a Race* in 1917. Wheeler's goal was to make films of Booker T. Washington's *Up From Slavery*, W.E.B. Du Bois's *The Quest of the Silver Fleece,* and novelist Charles Chestnut's *The House Behind the Cedars,* all narratives of African American advancement. Scott, of course, was most excited about the possibility of a film on the life of Booker T. Washington. He contacted E.L. Synder, a Chicago movie producer, asking him to assist Wheeler in filming the story.

The production of *Birth of a Race* began as a response to the virulently racist film *Birth of a Nation* by moviemaker D.W. Griffith. As *Birth of a Nation* stirred white antipathy toward black Americans, many African Americans campaigned to have the film banned. The leadership of the NAACP waged a fervid campaign to accomplish this goal.

Scott's strategy, derived from his Tuskegee background, was to counter the Griffith film with one showing the accomplishments of black Americans. This endeavor also was potentially profitable, so Scott hastened to meet with prominent movie executives, such as H.C. Oppenheimer of the Universal Film Company of New York. In his efforts to raise money, he helped incorporate the Birth of a Race Photoplay Company in Delaware. He turned again to Julius Rosenwald for financial assistance, hired the stock brokerage company of Giles P. Cory in Chicago, and recruited the famous African American baritone Harry T. Burleigh to compose and arrange music for the film. Scott was the main business force behind the production of *Birth of a Race.* That film eventually fell into obscurity, where it remained until its rediscovery in the 1970s, but it revealed the medium's possibilities for portraying African American life and achievements. By the mid-1920s, Scott and Wheeler had given up on the idea of making films about black life.[68]

Throughout his life, Scott promoted the cause of African American advancement through economic gain-even when that idea was increasingly seen as too narrow. With his special interest in the press, Scott saw how it, too, could serve the African American community. He used his elder statesman status to influence the editors of black newspapers. He publicized himself and his causes in important African American newspapers, such as the *Washington Bee,* the *New York Age,* the *Savannah Journal,* the *Wilmington Advocate,* and the *Pittsburgh Courier.* Many of the articles by Scott underscored his political, educational, and social agendas, such as his support of the Republican Party and Howard University.[69] Scott also used his influence with editors of the *Norfolk Journal and Guide* and the *Afro-*

American to draw attention to African American firms.[70]

Scott's final business venture was the Sun Shipbuilding Company of Chester, Pennsylvania. In 1941 Scott went to work at Sun Shipbuilding, supervising an African American labor yard that built tankers and cargo ships for the U.S. Maritime Commission during World War II.

When the war ended in 1945, the yard was dismantled and Scott retired to Washington, where he occasionally did public relations work. He died there in 1957. Always mindful of his image, Scott, with the help of a friend, had drafted his own obituary, which reminded readers of his glory days, working alongside Washington: "Adroitly, Dr. Washington and Dr. Scott flattered, cajoled, pleaded, and preached ... not only Negro education, but Negro journalism, Negro business, Negro fraternal [associations], the Negro church, and the Negro professional classes ...."[71]

Scott's life and activities in the realm of business are, on their face, difficult to summarize, because he was neither a phenomenal success nor an abject failure. He did not earn a large amount of investment income, nor did he leave behind a major commercial establishment that would reflect the goals of his generation of black capitalists and entrepreneurs. Yet there are lessons to be derived from his story. His mixed legacy is not dramatically different from that of many black capitalists and business promoters in the early twentieth century. He was, like all African American entrepreneurs, seriously hampered by a limited access to capital and by a small, relatively poor, customer base. But some of his difficulties were exacerbated by his own tendencies: *he* was often enamored of enterprising strivers and took on too many projects at once.

Nonetheless, Scott gave a voice and provided a vision to black talent in America, and his hard work, in some instances, produced concrete results: in Atlanta, where businessmen were able to build on the work of Heman Perry, whose success owed so much to Scott's support; in Mound Bayou, where the concept of business growth helped to sustain an all-black township; in the production of an early African American film; in the launching of a successful record company; and in the National Negro Business League, which flourished during the time of Scott's involvement. He was a pioneer whose imagination led him down many paths in his quest to build business opportunities for black Americans.

(Endnotes)

1   Maceo Crenshaw Dailey Jr., "Neither 'Uncle Tom' nor 'Accommodationist': Booker T. Washington, Emmett Jay Scott, and Constructionalism," *Atlanta History: A Journal of Georgia and the South* 37 (Winter 1995): 20-34; also, Maceo Crenshaw Dailey Jr., "An Easy Alliance: Theodore Roosevelt and Emmett Jay Scott, 1900-1919," in Theodore *Roosevelt: Many-Sided American*, eds. Natalie A Naylor, Douglas Brinkley, and John Allen Gable (New York, 1992); August Meier, *Negro Thought In America, 1880-1915: Racial Ideology* in *the Age of Booker T. Washington* (Ann Arbor, Mich., 1973), 139-57.

2   Maceo Crenshaw Dailey Jr., "Emmett Jay Scott: The Career of a Secondary Black Leader (Ph.D. diss., Howard University, 1983), 1-34.

3   Ibid., 1-34, 372-6. Several sources provide information on the early years of Scott's life: "Remarks of Dr. Emmett Jan Scott Upon the Occasion of His Declared Intention to Bequeath to Morgan State College His Library Collection, Personal Papers, etc.," presented to the Morgan State University Library in Baltimore on 30 April 1952, a copy of which is located in the Special Portfolio of Office Files in the Davis Room of the Library; Scott's obituary in the *New York Times*, 14 Dec. 1957; Emmett Jay Scott, Autobiographical Writings, n.d., cont. 7, in the Emmett Jay Scott Papers; Rayford W. Logan and Michael R. Winston, *Dictionary of American Negro Biography* (New York, 1982), 151-2.

4   Louis Harlan, *Booker T. Washington:* The *Making of a Black Leader, 1856-1901* (New York, 1972).

5   Published in New York by D. Appleton. For a brief overview of Scott's career, see Edgar Allan Toppin, "Scott, Emmett Jay," in John A Garraty and Mark C. Carnes, *American National Biography* (New York, 1999).

6   Dailey, "Emmett Jay Scott," 1-34, 35-65.

7   See Harlan, *Booker T. Washington*, 266-8; Emma Lou Thornbrough, *T. Thomas Fortune: Militant Journalist* (Chicago, 1972), 202; David Levering Lewis, *W. E. B. Du Bois: Biography of a Race, 1868-1919* (New York, 1993), 240.

8   Telephone conversations with Kenneth Hamilton, 8 May and 19 Apr. 2002.

9   Dailey, "Emmett Jay Scott," 228-30. The figures for the NNBL membership come from Emmett Jay Scott and Lyman Beecher Stowe, *Booker T. Washington: Builder of a Civilization* (Garden City, N.Y., 1916), 192-3.

10   Dailey, "Emmett Jay Scott," 183-84, 197-236, 317-18; Julius Rosenwald to Mrs. Rosenwald, 12 Nov. 1915, in the Rosenwald Papers, Box BLIV, University of Chicago.

11   *Chicago Inter-Ocean*, 27 Sept. 1911, 20 Feb. 1913, Rosenwald Papers, Boxes BLIII, BLIV, University of Chicago.

12   Louis R. Harlan, *Booker T. Washington: The Wizard of Tuskegee, 1901-1915* (New York, 1983), xi-xii.

13   Ibid.

14   Ibid.

15   Dailey, "Emmett Jay Scott," 261-2.

16   Scott to R. E. Jones, 2 Aug. 1919, cont. 18, Emmett Jay Scott Papers, Soper Library, Morgan State University, Baltimore (hereafter Scott Papers).

17   NNBL Brochure, n.d., National Negro Business League Papers, Collection no. 1434, Box 7, Special Collections Library, University of California, Los Angeles; Scott to R. E. Jones, 2 Aug. 1919, cont. 18; Scott to B. J. Davis, 12 Apr. 1920, cont. 16; Scott to James H. Durbin, 8 Apr. 1920, cont. 16; Scott to William L. Houston, 8 Apr. 1920, cont. 17, Scott Papers; Burrows, "The Necessity of Myth," 135; Dailey, "Emmett Jay Scott," 330-2.

18   Dailey, "Emmett Jay Scott," 261-2, 335-43. The remaining three letters between Scott, Spaulding, and Jones revealed Scott's plans to resign from the NNBL. See Scott to Charles C. Spaulding, 8 Sept. 1922, cont. 29; Spaulding to Scott, 6 May 1922, cont. 29; Scott to R. E. Jones, 20 Dec. 1922, cont. 27-all in Scott Papers.

19   Published in Chicago by the Homewood Press.

20   Dailey, "Emmett Jay Scott," 306-9; *Crisis* 18 (May 1919): 10; *Crisis* 18 (July 1919): 129.

21   Ibid., 263-318, 371; Emmett Jay Scott, *Official History of the American Negro* in *the World War* (New York, 1969 [1919]).

22   Monroe N. Work, "A Half Century of Progress: The Negro in American in 1866 and 1922," *Missionary Review of the World* 45 (June 1922): 431-40.

23   E. William to Scott, 18 Jan. 1920, cont. 31, Emmett Jay Scott Papers, Soper Library, Morgan State University, Baltimore; James Waller, "Emmett Jay Scott: The Public Life of a Private Secretary" (M.A thesis, University of Maryland, 1971); William E. Leuchtenburg, The *Perils of Prosperity, 1914-32* (Chicago, 1958), 9, 188; Abram L. Harris, The *Negro as Capitalist: A Study of Banking and Business among American Negroes* (Philadelphia, 1936); Work, A Half Century of Progress," 431-40; August Meier, *A White Scholar and the Black Community, 1945-1965* (Amherst, Mass., 1992), 91.

24   Meier, *A White Scholar*, 91.

25   Dailey, "Emmett Jay Scott, 197.

26 Juliet E. K. Walker, The *History of Black Business in America: Capitalism, Race, Entrepreneurship* (New York, 1998), 86,189-90.

27 Scott *to* E. William, 19 Sept. 1923, cont. 29; E. William *to* Scott, 19 Sept. 1923, cont. 29; Scott to Rucker, 12 Jan. 1920, cont. 20; Scott to H. C. Dugas, 24 Jan. 1920, cont. 16; Ferguson to Scott, 2 July 1921, cont. 26; Scott to Ferguson, 9 Jan. 1921, cont. 26; Scott to Perry, 28 July 1919, cont. 21, Scott Papers.

28 Dailey, "Emmett Jay Scott," 219-20, 320-7; Alexa Benson Henderson, *Atlanta Life Insurance Company: Guardian of Black Economic Dignity* (Tuscaloosa, Ala., 1990), 57-9. See St. Clair Drake and Horace R. Cayton, *Black Metropolis: A Study of Negro Life in A Northern City* (New York, 1945), 394: "The term 'Race Man' is used in a dual sense .... It refers to any person who has a reputation as an uncompromising fighter against attempts to subordinate Negroes. It is also used in a derogatory sense to refer to people who pay loud lip-service to 'race pride.'"

29 Judy Simmons, "Heman Perry, the Commercial Booker Washington," *Black Enterprise*, Apr. 1978, 45; C. L Henton, "Heman Perry: Documentary Materials for the Life of a Businessman" (M.A. thesis, Clark Atlanta University, 1948), 273; Alexa Benson Henderson, "Heman E. Perry and Black Enterprise in Atlanta, 1908-1925," *Business History Review* 61 (Spring 1987): 221; Carter G. Woodson, "Insurance Business among Negroes," *Journal of Negro History* 14 (Apr. 1929): 216-17; Henderson, *Atlanta Life Insurance Company*, 57-9; 100-4.

30 Henton, "Heman Perry," 276-82; Henderson, "Heman E. Perry," 229.

31 Henton, "Heman Perry," 273; Henderson, "Heman E. Perry," 221; Woodson, "Insurance Business," 216-17; W. E. B. Du Bois, The *Ordeal* of Mansart (New York, 1957), 288-9, and *Mansart Builds a School* (New York, 1959), 164-6; 170-74. Both books are in a trilogy by Du Bois, The *Black Flame*.

32 Edyth Williams to Scott, 18 Jan. 1920, cont. 31, Scott Papers; Dailey, "Emmett Jay Scott," 320-8.

33 Dailey, "Emmett Jay Scott," 218-20.

34 Henton, "Heman Perry, • 273; Henderson, "Heman E. Perry, 224.

35 Quote is from Scott to Perry, 11 Sept. 1922, cont. 28. See also Scott to Perry, 31 Aug. 1922, cont. 28; Scott to Perry, 9 July 1923, cont. 33; Scott to Ferguson, 25 Jan. 1923, cont. 32, Perry to Scott, 9 Mar. 1922, cont. 29, Scott Papers.

36 Scott to Ferguson, 25 Jan. 1923, cont. 32; Scott to Perry, 9 July 1923, cont. 33; Scott to Perry, 31 Aug. 1922, cont. 29; see Scott's rough draft of article, "Negro Capitalists Gather in Atlanta," c. 1923, cont. 33; Perry to Scott, 9 Mar. 1922, cont. 29; Scott to Perry, 11 Sept. 1922, cont. 28, Scott Papers.

37 Figures were taken from Henderson, "Heman Perry, • 229, and Scott, "Negro Capitalists Gather in Atlanta." See also Scott to Ferguson, 14 Jan. 1923, cont. 29; Ferguson to Scott, 13 Jan. 1923, cont. 32; Scott to Ferguson, 5 Apr. 1924, cont. 2s; Perry to Scott, 5 Apr. 1924, cont. 25; Scott to Perry, 5 Apr. 1924, cont. 25; Scott to Perry, 17 Sept. 1923, cont. 28; Scott to Perry, 2 May 1922, cont. 29; Scott to Perry, 29 Mar. 1923, cont. 29, Scott Papers; W. E. B. Du Bois, The *Autobiography of W. E. B. Du*

Bois: *A Soliloquy on Viewing My Life from the Last Decade of its First Century* (New York, 1968), 277-88.

38   Dailey, "Emmett Jay Scott," 320-7.

39   Quote is taken from Scott's rough draft of the essay, "Negro Capitalists Gather in Atlanta," cont. 33- See also Scott to Perry, 9 July 1923, cont. 33; Scott to Perry, 3 Mar. 1923, cont. 29; Scott to Ferguson, 28 June 1923, cont. 29, Scott Papers; Dailey, "Emmett Jay Scott," 320-7.

40   Alexa B. Henderson, "Perry, Heman Edward," in Mark Carnes and John Garraty, *American National Biography* (New York:, 1999).

41   Comment about Du Bois was made by David L. Lewis in a telephone interview on 1 Feb. 1999; Scott to John B. Snowden, 7 Dec. 1921, cont. 21; Scott to John E. Nail, 25 Mar. 1922, cont. 28; Scott to J. F. Holland, 21 Jan. 1922, cont. 26; Pace to Scott, 25 Oct. 1921, cont. 28, Scott Papers; Dittmer, 46, 189.

42   Scott to E. C. Brown, 8 July 1922, cont. 23; Scott to Cobb, 21 Jan. 1922, cont. 24; Scott To W. T. Dalmage, 7 Jan. 1921, cont. 25; Scott to Nan, 14 Jan. 1923, cont. 28; Scott to Stephen Ridgeley, 24 June 1923, cont. 29; Scott to Perry, 20 Mar. 1923, cont. 29; C. A. Barnett to Scott, 24 Jan. 1922, cont. 23; Scott to Perry, 11 Oct. 1921, cont. 28, Scott Papers.

43   Dailey, "Emmett Jay Scott," 320-7.

44   Henton, Heman Perry," 282.

45   Scott to Ferguson, 14 Jan. 1923, cont. 29; Ferguson to Scott, 13 Jan. 1923, cont. 32; Scott to Ferguson, 5 Apr. 1924, cont. 2s; Perry to Scott, 5 Apr. 1924, cont. 25; Scott to Perry, 5 Apr. 1924, cont. 25; Scott to Perry, 17 Sept. 1923, cont. 28; Scott to Perry, 2 May 1922, cont. 29; Scott to Perry, 29 Mar. 1923, cont. 29; Scott to Perry, 2 May 1922, cont. 29; Scott to Perry, 29 Mar. 1923, cont. 29, Scott Papers; John Dittmer, *Black Georgia in the Progressive Era, 1900-1920* (Urbana, Ill, 1977), 46-7.

46   John N. Ingham and Lynne B. Feldman, *African American Business Leaders: A Biographical Dictionary* (Westport, Conn., 1994), 542.

47   Henderson, *Atlanta Life Insurance Company*, 103-13.

48   Dittmer, *Black Georgia*, 46-7.

49   Ibid.; Simmons, "Heman Perry," 42- 8; Henderson, "Heman E. Perry," 221-9.

50   *Leadership and Black Higher Education in the Early Twentieth Century* (Athens, Ga., 1998), 275-6. Hope wanted the Rosenwald Foundation to provide $200,000 to prevent a white company from taking over Standard Life. Davis describes Hope's activities to save the black company as being couched in a "nationalist framework."

51   Woodson, "Insurance Business among Negroes," 216-26; Henderson, *Atlanta Life Insurance Company*, 101-13; Dittmer, *Black Georgia*, 46-7.

52   Henderson, "Perry, Heman Edward."

6666666

22222222

1222222

333333

222222

53 Scott to E. C. Brown, 8 July 1922, cont. 23; Scott to Cobb, 21 Jan. 1922, cont. 24; Scott to W. T. Dalmage, 7 Jan. 1921, cont. 25; Scott to Nail, 14 Jan. 1923, cont. 28; Scott to Stephen Ridgeley, 24 June 1923, cont. 29; Scott to Perry, 20 Mar. 1923, cont. 29; C. A. Barnett to Scott, 24 Jan. 1922, cont. 23; Scott to Perry, 11 Oct. 1921, cont. 28, Scott Papers.

54 Waller, "Emmett Jay Scott," 35; Louis R. Harlan and Raymond Smock, *The Booker T. Washington Papers,* vol. 12 (Urbana, Ill., 1982), 30-1.

55 Scott to Charles Chappelle, 1 Dec. 1921, cont. 24; Chappelle to Scott, 1 Dec. 1921, cont. 24; Chappelle to Scott, 1 Dec. 1921, cont. 24; Scott to President of Levison Company, 20 Dec. 1921, cont. 24; President of Levison Company to Scott, 27 Dec. 1921, cont. 27, Scott Papers.

56 Scott to Cobb, 9 Nov. 1921, cont. 24; Chappelle to Scott, 1 Dec. 1921, cont. 24; Chappelle to Scott, 5 Dec. 1921, cont. 24; Scott to Frank, 8 Dec. 1921, cont. 26, Scott Papers.

57 Banks to R. E. Jones, 10 Sept. 1919, cont. 14; Scott to Banks, 29 Sept. 1919, cont. 15; Scott to Banks, 29 Oct. 1919, cont. 14; Scott to Lewis, 12 Dec. 1919, cont. 18; Scott to Kyle, 16 Dec. 1919, cont. 18; Banks to Scott, 1 Jan. 1920, cont. 14, Scott Papers.

58 Banks to Moore, 13 Jan. 1920, cont. 15; Scott to Banks, 20 Jan. 1920, cont. 15; Scott to Isaiah Montgomery, 28 Jan. 1920, cont. 21, Scott Papers.

59 Banks to Scott, 8 May 1922, cont. 23; Booze to R. J. Gear, c. 1922, cont. 23; A. W. McLean to Booze, 12 May 1922, cont. 23; Banks to Scott, 8 May 1922, cont. 23; Booze to Scott, 12 May 1922, cont. 23, Scott Papers.

60 Ibid.

61 See David Jackson, *A Chief Lieutenant of the Tuskegee Machine: Charles Banks of Mississippi* (Gainesville, Fla., 2002), for a discussion of the life of Banks and his role as a supporter of Scott and Washington.

62 Dailey, ·Emmett Jay Scott, · 359-60; Pace to Scott, 21 Oct. 1921, cont. 28; Pace to Scott, 8 October 1920, cont. 26; Pace to Scott, 5 Nov. 1921, cont. 28; Scott to Holsey, 19 Mar. 1920, cont. 17; Scott to Pace, 30 Nov. 1921, cont. 28, Scott Papers.

63 Scott to Pace, 3 Mar. 1922, cont. 28; Pace to Scott, 13 Apr. 1920, cont. 17; Scott to I. S. Rosenfels, 16 March 1920, cont. 20, Scott Papers.

64 Robert Weems Jr., *Desegregating the Dollar: African American Consumerism in the Twentieth Century* (New York, 1998), 16.

65 C. A. Barnett to Scott, 24 Aug. 1921, cont. 23, Scott Papers.

66 C. A. Barnett to Scott, 24 Aug. 1921, cont. 23; Lyman Beecher Stowe to Scott, 27 Dec. 1937, cont. 60; Scott to Raymond Murray, 26 Oct. 1921, cont. 27; Scott to S. H. Dudley and R. H. Murray, 7 Mar. 1922, cont. 25; Scott to Stowe, 15 July 1943, cont. 64; Scott to Stowe, 3 Jan. 1938, cont. 60; Scott to Stowe, 15 July 1943, cont. 64; Essie Robeson to Scott, 6 Nov. 1944, cont. 68; Scott to Essie Robeson, 9 Nov. 1944, cont. 68; Scott to Essie Robeson, 4 Nov. 1944, cont. 68; Ben Tallon to Scott, 28 Apr. 1934, cont. 44, Scott Papers.

67 Scott to William R. Cowan, 3 Feb. 1920, cont. 24; Scott to Oscar Micheaux, 10 Apr. 1920, cont. 19, Scott Papers.

68   Wheeler to Scott, 10 Apr. 1920, cont. 31; Wheeler to Scott, 6 Feb. 1920, cont. 31; Wheeler to Scott, 20 July 1921, cont. 31; Scott to Wheeler, 6 Aug. 1921, cont. 31; Scott to E. L. Grafton, 14 July 1921, cont. 26; Ransom to Scott, 17 Apr. 1920, cont. 20; Scott to Wheeler, 21 Jan. 1920, cont. 31; Wheeler to Scott, 2 Feb. 1920, cont. 31; Scott to Wheeler, 15 Apr. 1920, cont. 31, Scott Papers.

69   B. J. Davis to Scott, 1 Mar. 1920, cont. 14; Scott to Abbott, 28 Feb. 1920, cont. 14; Scott to Calvin Chase, 28 Feb. 1920, cont. 25; Scott to Barnett, 28 Feb. 1920, cont. 15; Scott to R. Tyler, 28 Feb. 1920, cont. 22, Scott Papers.

70   Ransom to Scott, 26 Jan. 1920, cont. 20; Scott to Ransom, 29 Jan. 1920, cont. 20; Perry to Scott, 19 Sept. 1921, cont. 28; Scott to Calvin Chase, 28 Feb. 1920, cont. 14; Scott to Abbott, 28 Feb. 1920, cont. 14; Scott to C. A. Barnett, 28 Feb. 1920, cont. 15, Scott Papers.

71   Emmett Jay Scott, Autobiographical Writings, n.d., cont. 7, Scott Papers, Maceo Crenshaw Dailey Jr., Interview with Alfred Smith, Washington, D.C., 24 Nov. 1981.

INDEX